The Enjoyment of Face Reading and Palmistry

光酉時小吉戌辭送亥從魁子河魁丑登明寅辰后卯
然後斷之右前○起制掌訣
值空亡日時則爲不驗
正九丑上起初一二
起例掌訣
午未二子
巳辰卯寅戌亥
正月初一丑初二寅初
位是丑巳位是是午上吉
宮上退一位到午上便

World Publishing Co.

The Enjoyment of
Face Reading and Palmistry

Author:
Peter So Man Fung

Editor:
Sharmon Choy

Translator:
John Lee Wei Kin

Designer:
Paul Suen

Illustrator:
Ken Wong Man Kin

Photographer:
Polerstar advertising co.

Published by:
World Publishing Co.
14/F., Tsuen Wan Industrial Centre, 220-248 Texaco Rd.,
Tsuen Wan, N.T. Hong Kong.
Tel: 2408 8801

Printed by:
Fook Hing Offset Printing Co. Ltd.

Sole agency (Hong Kong):
World Publishing Co.
14/F., Tsuen Wan Industrial Centre, 220-248 Texaco Rd.,
Tsuen Wan, N.T. Hong Kong.
Tel: 2408 8801

Sole agency (Singapore):
Popular Book Co. (PTE) LTD.
20 Old Toh Tuck Road, Singapore 597655
Tel: (S) 6338 2323 Fax: (S) 6468 3710

Sole agency (Malaysia):
Popular Book Co. (M) SDN. BHD.
No. 8, Jalan 7/118B, Desa Tun Razak,
56000 Kuala Lumpur, Malaysia
Tel: 03-9179 6333 Fax: 03-9179 6063

Published in *January, 2004*
Copyright©2004 World Publishing Co. /
Popular Book Co. (PTE) LTD. /
Popular Book Co. (M) SDN.BHD.
All rights reserved.

FOREWORD

Being a fortune teller, I am posed with endless questions on face and palm reading every day. That's how I came up with the idea of compiling all "most requested" topics presented in humourous ways and written into fun-filled short writings.

This book is a collection of such writings in which you find headings that make you smile and information that fulfills the nosy side of your curiosity. Of course, this book is undeniably practical and hands-on. I honestly hope my readers have fun reading it in leisure time while still making some serious knowledge about fortune telling and hence, getting benefits from it.

-- Peter So Man-fung

CHRONOLOGY

P eter So Man-fung: long haired, born in 1960, nick named Modern Lai Bu-yi, has unique views on Feng Shui and geomancy. He has incredible talent and immediacy on geomancy so that he always derives the accurate reading instantly.

1983: started amateur meetings with clients to build up experience.

1986: started teaching face/palm reading and Hexagram theory (not So Clan theory).

1987: left for a 6-month trip to Tibet. He visited all the Buddhist sacred sites in Tibet and extensively experienced the life there. Much enlightened by this trip, Peter So came back to Hong Kong and opened stores selling Tibetian Buddhist worship items and daily utensils. He also started semi-professional palm and face reading in those stores.

1988: left for a Feng Shui trip to Northern Europe, ranging from Sweden, Norway, Denmark in the North to Spain in the South. He was hired to give Feng Shui advice in Canada in the same year. Peter was interviewed by Variety Magazine.

1989: went to Canada and United States again to serve the Chinese community there. He also took up overseas assignments in Singapore, Japan and Taiwan. He was interviewed by City Magazine that year.

1990: went twice to North America and a few times to Taiwan. He got many interviews from the Taiwanese press, including Jade Magazine and Life Daily. In the same year, Peter took up 3 students to teach them So Clan Feng Shui.

1991: continued his visits to Canada, United States and Taiwan. This year he got interviewed by Express Daily, ATV and BBC (Britain). All interviews were conducted on the subject of how Feng Shui affects our life, in a view to encourage the audience to deal with their life more actively. Peter also released his first video recording: "The Introduction to Feng Shui, a scrapbook by modern Lai Bu-yi."

1992: more trips to North America and South East Asia this year. His interview with BBC got broadcast in various English speaking TV channels, including Star TV. Peter started his first class to teach solely So Clan Feng Shui.

1994: flew to the Southern hemisphere for a Feng Shui trip for the first time to find that the calculation and methodology of Geomancy in Australia to be different from that of Northern hemisphere. This was regarded as an important finding in the Feng Shui industry. Peter got interviewed by 2 geomancy magazines "Shocking mysteries" and "Legends"

1995: re-released the video "The introduction to Feng Shui". He got interviewed by Sing Tao Daily News and Sing Tao Evening News.

1996: hired to give Feng Shui advice in Australia, San Francisco, Hawaii, Taiwan and other South East Asian countries. Peter was interviewed by Outstanding Weekly, Easy Finder, Penthouse, The Associated Press and MTV.

1997: went to South Africa on an assignment for the first time. He got interviewed by NHK Japan, a terrestrial TV in Denmark,

Property Times, Fortune & Investment Magazine and Sing Pao Daily. He invented Five-Element Counteracting Resolution against real estate Feng Shui traps.

1998: went to Italy and Britain for Feng Shui assignments. This year Peter was interviewed by TVB Weekly, B International and Next Magazine. He was also invited to be a guest host on Cable TV, Metro Broadcast and Commercial Radio.

1999: went to Europe for Feng Shui assignments. More interviews were conducted in press and various electronic media including Next Magazine, East Weekly and The Sun. He also co-hosted many shows on several radio and TV channels. He published "Essential Face Reading"(chinese version) and released a collection of Feng Shui diamond jewelry, namely Five Elements Series, Yin and Yang Series and Round Sky Square Earth Series. He was then interviewed by many on the subject of Feng Shui jewelry.

2000: went to Europe and the U.S. again for Feng Shui assignments. He went to New York City for the first time and posted his first website masterso.com. Many magazines interviewed him on the content of the website and he also got interviewed by university student magazine Varsity, Japanese edition of Marie Claire, Top 100 bright persons from Hong Kong published by Rehab Power, Esquire, Ming Pao Weekly etc. He also published his first book on Feng Shui — "Feng Shui Made Easy: The book of Household Setting" and first book on general luck in that individual year "Luck in the Year of the

Snake". He came up with another series of Feng Shui diamond accessories in the same year. He co-hosted more shows on TVB, Commercial Radio and Metro Broadcast.

2001: went to Europe for Feng Shui assignments again. He also got interviewed by South China Morning Post, Sudden Weekly, Apple Daily, Japanese magazine Hanujikan; Japanese national terrestrial TV NHK; regional TV KTV at Kansai, Japan; and Japanese national Daily Yomiuri. He co-hosted programs on the Chinese radio station in New York. He published his second Feng Shui book — "Feng Shui Made Easy: The book of Directions and Dates of Birth" and his second book on luck of that individual year "Luck in the Year of the Horse."

2002: went once again to Europe for Feng Shui assignments and co-hosted again on the Chinese radio in New York. He also co-hosted shows on RTHK and published this book "The Enjoyment of Face Reading and Palmisty"(Chinese version).

Master So Consultancy

Room 4, 12/F, Rightful Centre, 11 - 12 Tak Hing Street, Kowloon

Tel: 2780 3675   Fax: 2780 1489

Website: http://www.masterso.com

Appointment and meeting schedule: Mon to Sat from 2 pm to 7 pm

CONTENT

Section 3 Knowing the Right People — 133

Section 4 Resolving Bad Luck — 233

Section 1
Love and Marriage

1. When will I get married?

You wait and wait. You still don't know when you will meet the right one to be with you for the rest of your life. Actually, you can deduce roughly when you will meet someone who loves you. Of course, that one who loves you might as well marry you. Then read the marriage line on your palm to determine which relationship is most likely to be your marriage.

■ The year of love affairs for various Chinese zodiac sign

Rat — 2005, 2008, 2014   Horse — 2005, 2011, 2017

Ox — 2002, 2004, 2010   Goat — 2004, 2008, 2010

Tiger — 2003, 2011, 2009   Monkey — 2003, 2005, 2009

Rabbit — 2002, 2008, 2014   Rooster — 2002, 2008, 2014

Dragon — 2005, 2007, 2013   Dog — 2007, 2011, 2013

Snake — 2002, 2006, 2012   Pig — 2006, 2008, 2012

Add 12 (or 24, or 36···) to these years for the next cycle.

Remember, you will only meet someone who loves you in the year of love affairs corresponding to your zodiac sign, but he/she is not necessarily someone you love. That's why people always miss these possible love affairs as they don't pay attention to those they are not attracted to.

■ *Read the signs of love*

The colour and tone of a person's face tell if he/she is already in love:

1. The eyes suddenly turn bright and shiny, with a look of high spirit. They also look watery and glossy.

2. He/she always smiles and becomes easy going.

3. The cheeks are pink without drinking alcohol.

4. The line of love relationships becomes shiny.

■ *Read the palm for the year of marriage*

The lines below the small finger and above the line of love relationships are called lines of marriage. They tell when a person meets someone important and have deep relationship, and possibly getting married with him/her.

Lines of marriage can be of different length and depth. Deep and long lines mean stronger and more intense relationships while light and short lines mean weaker relationships.

In case you have a long marriage line matching one of your years of love affairs (according to your zodiac sign), that certain relationship is more likely to turn into marriage.

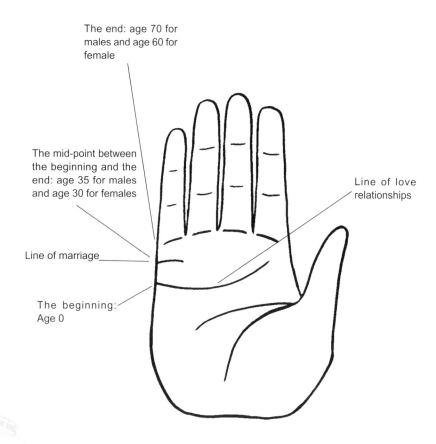

The end: age 70 for males and age 60 for female

The mid-point between the beginning and the end: age 35 for males and age 30 for females

Line of love relationships

Line of marriage

The beginning: Age 0

A palm shows line of marriage and line of love relationships

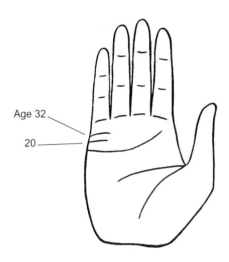

Female's palm

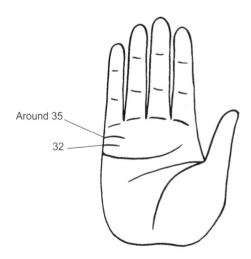

Male's palm

2. How do you tell good marriages from bad ones?

Take a look at a mirror or your palm and you'll know whether you'll have good or bad marriage.

■ Read it on the face

Luck of marriage can be deduced by the cheekbones, nose and the outer eye corners.

Nose — For both sexes, a tall straight nose-bridge without any mole, line or scar means the person can get assistance from the opposite sex and have good luck of marriage. Yet, those with big and tall nose but low skinny cheekbones are exceptions.

A man with a big tall nose but low skinny cheekbones is usually difficult to get along with. He also has poor relationships with sons and daughters. Yet, he still has a good marriage with a gentle wife who let him take control of everything.

A woman with a big tall nose but low skinny cheekbones is prone to marriage problems, or else she is likely to remain single all her life. Such woman is highly self-centred and too confident. She is likely to look down on most men and thinks she deserves something better. Time passes and she would miss the chances and be single. Even if she finds a good husband, they are still likely to divorce in the end due to intensive arguments.

A woman with a low depressed nose-bridge, despite good relationship with and good influence on luck by sons and daughters, usually has bad luck of marriage. The only way out is to marry someone beyond "regular practice", say, someone at least 10 years older than herself, or marrying someone younger than herself, or marrying someone abroad, or marrying a widowed man. In those cases, the woman has good marriage luck and except in the case of younger husband, the wife's luck is also enhanced by the husband. On the other hand, if the woman marries a "regular" husband (i.e. just a few years older than she is), he is either an alcoholic or he visits prostitutes on regular basis.

A man with a low nose-bridge only means his wife would not of much help in terms of luck and career. As people tend to think it's only natural a woman cannot help, it is not considered a very bad sign.

Flaws like moles, lines and scars on the nose-bridge usually mean poor spousal relationship, or poor health, or frequent arguments. Pay special attention to these aspects at age 20, 29, 38, 41 and 44.

Cheekbones — This is the reading point to tell if a woman helps her husband's luck or adversely affects her husband's luck. Generally speaking, a woman who has a tall nose and high fleshy cheekbones enhances the husband's luck and benefits from his success. A woman with low nose-bridge and high fleshy cheekbones enhances the husband's luck without enjoying the benefits from his success. A woman with skinny protruding cheekbones adversely affects her husband's luck. If she also has a high protruding forehead, the influence is even worse.

On the contrary, cheekbones do not say much about a man's marriage.

Outer eye corners ── These are the areas of spousal relationship. Fullness without any mole around the outer eye corners that are not pointing downwards means good spousal relationship.

Moles around the outer eye corners mean the spousal relationship is so-so. If the mole is on the left side, it means the husband has poor health. A mole around the outer eye corner on the right side means the wife has poor health. Outer eye corners pointing downward are even worse as they imply the possibility of divorce. This is especially true to females and the problem usually arises at age 39 and 40. Also pay attention to spousal relationship at age 23, 26, 32 and 35.

■ *Read it on the palm*

The lines of marriage and lines of love relationships also tell whether your marriage is good or not.

The line of love relationships — A good one should be long and curving (concave) upward and ending below the base of the index finger. (See Fig 1) It means the person is enthusiastic to commit in relationships and willing to accept the shortcomings of his/her partner. The line might split into 2 or 3 lines in the end (See Fig2, Fig3)and this is a good sign as splitting into 2 means the good love relationship while splitting into 3 means wealthy life together with the loved one.

On the other hand, a line of love relationships that curves (concave) downward (See Fig 4) or one that is broken (See Fig 5) means the person will encounter many frustrations in love relationships, such as cheating on each other. He/she is unlikely to have good marriage.

Fig 1: Long and curving upward

Fig 2: The end splits into 2 lines

Fig 3: The end splits into 3 lines

Fig 4: A line curving downward is called the line of disappointment

Fig 5: A broken line means breaking up at that point of life

Fig 6: A short line means the person dares not commit to relationships

The lines of marriage — These are the fine lines below the base of the small finger and above the beginning of the line of love relationships. They are horizontal to the palm and go around the edge of the palm. Good ones should be long and deep. Short, shallow, or broken ones or those with islets, split ends, pointing downward or pointing upward are all considered bad.

Please note that male readers should look at their left palms while female readers should look at their right ones.

One or two long and deep lines of marriage running parallel mean happy marriage.

Normal line of marriage

If a line of marriage is broken, it means a divorce.

Broken line of marriage

A person having many short lines of marriage without a deep and long one might not have any relationship worth turning into marriage in his/her life. Even if he/she gets married, the spousal relationship remains very shallow and detached.

Short lines of marriage

Light lines of marriage mean the person does not have passion for marriage. If he/she gets married without believing in the system, he/she will end up in a divorce.

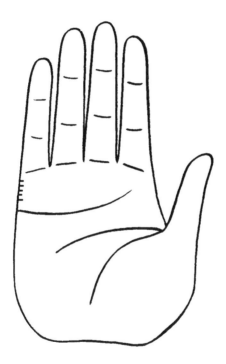

Light (shallow) lines of marriage

Islets on the lines of marriage mean barriers and particular difficult times for the relationship. If the islet is in the beginning (i.e. close to the edge of the palm) of the line of marriage, the person can overcome the difficulty and have good marriage after that.

If the islet happens to be at the end (i.e. closer to the centre of the palm) of the line of marriage, the person might not be able to solve the problems and might break up with his/her partner in the end.

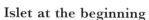

Islet at the beginning   **Islet at the end**

Split ends mean major disagreement between husband and wife or the two of them are separated in two different countries for a long time.

A line of marriage with split ends

A line of marriage that goes upward or downward means the couple either does not have good relationship or both of them are prone to sickness after marriage.

A line of marriage that goes downward

A line of marriage that goes upward

3. Palm reading on the luck of love

People fitting into different archetypal palm shapes have different personalities.

Primitive Palm — Such palm is thick, big, coarse and stiff. The fingers are short and there are not many lines on the palm. People with such palm focus on gratification of personal desires and sex without deep thoughts. They have high sex drive like primitive people. They do not make very good dating material as they are dry, shallow, uncreative, and they do things the same way every time. Yet, such people would take responsibility in a family and are tough hard workers.

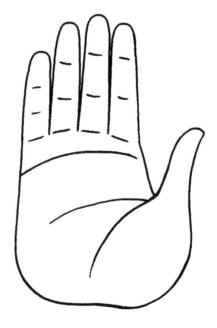

Philosopher's Palm — Such palm is square in shape, with the right thickness. It is slightly on the soft side without much flesh. The key features are the bulging joints and wide gap between the fingers.

Such people are analytical and determined to find answers to questions. They are committed in love relationship and would surprise the partners once in a while. Yet, they are not keen on sex and they only pursue spiritual fulfillment.

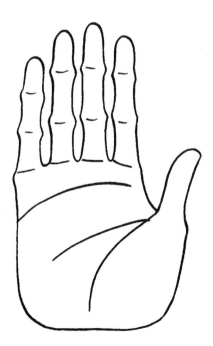

Round Palm — It is thick, round, fleshy, resilient and slightly red in colour. The fingers are fat like long cones. People with such palm have good interpersonal skills, like to please others and have excellent luck with the opposite sex.

They are imaginative and sometimes artistic. Yet, they are unlikely to get involved in arguments and fights associated with love affairs.

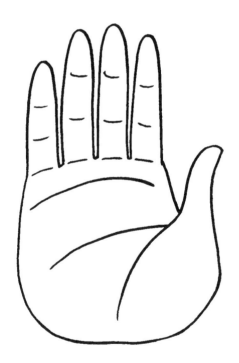

Dreamer's Palm — It is close to a philosopher's palm but even longer in shape with more slender fingers like chicken feet. Such people are sheer dreamers without much action.

They are impractical and even if they meet someone they like, they keep that liking in mind without acting out. They might just end up single all their lives.

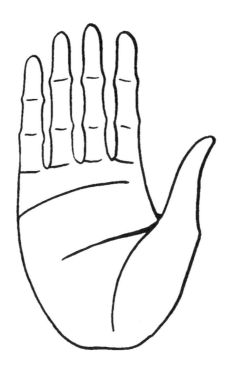

Pointy Palm — It is narrow and thin with pointy slender fingers without bulging joints. (See Fig 7) The palm can be slightly red or white in colour. People having such thought-type palms are sensitive, sentimental, dependent, shy and they need protection. That is why most people having such palms are female.

Square Palm — The palm is wide with the slightly square finger tips. (See Fig 8) Such people are square and follow the same route all their lives. They have the same view on love affairs which means they are very loyal, but boring partners.

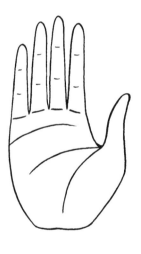

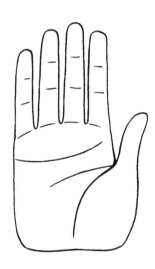

Fig 7   **Fig 8**

Besides the palm, the fingers also tell a person's character. Long thumb means stamina and endurance. Yet, a thumb too long means the person has abusive character. Long index finger means the person likes to take control and order others around. Long ring finger means the person is very accommodating in terms of others' requests. Long small finger means the person is incredulous and suspicious.

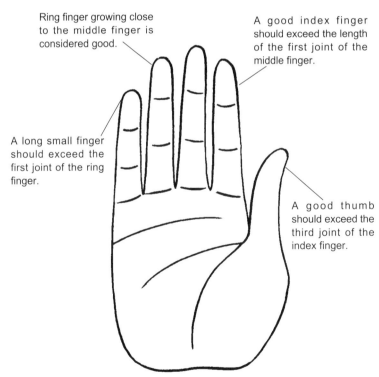

Ring finger growing close to the middle finger is considered good.

A good index finger should exceed the length of the first joint of the middle finger.

A long small finger should exceed the first joint of the ring finger.

A good thumb should exceed the third joint of the index finger.

4. A woman who enhances husband's luck and benefits from husband's success

Women with such readings have good marriage luck. Their husbands will get more and more successful after marriage and such women do not have to worry about money and food. They can just sit back and enjoy the husbands' success.

Forehead — Such woman has a wide full forehead a little higher than normal. She has good luck in the youth ages and her husband will succeed at a relatively young age. Low forehead means she has bad luck in the youth ages while a forehead too high means she is incompatible with her husband and has detached relationship with him.

Hair — Soft and fine hair represents gentleness and artistic thinking. She is likely to yield to her husband's view in times of argument and put an end to unnecessary conflict. That explains the good spousal relationship.

Eyebrows — Such woman has neatly grown eyebrows. Inner eye brow ends reflect sentiments while the outer ones reflect thinking. Neat eyebrows mean stable mood and clear thoughts, which in turn mean the woman would not bring more problems to the husband and her husband can then focus on work.

Cheekbones — Her cheekbones are slightly higher but fleshy, which is a sign of good luck to her husband. Bony protruding cheekbones are bad signs.

Mouth — A good mouth should be slightly smaller than normal and red in colour. Small mouth means the woman can stay in her position without challenging the authority of the husband. Red lips mean she has a healthy body with good circulation. Red lips are also signs of wealth and fame.

Eyes — Long slender eyes with big eyeballs and a high-spirit look are signs of wealth. Big eyeballs also mean the woman is kind and gentle in character. A high-spirit look in the eyes mean clear thinking, decisiveness and free from unnecessary worries.

Nose — Long straight nose-bridge slightly taller than normal is the best. A nose too tall means poor relationship with the husband. The nose is the location of husband luck for women and a long straight tall nose means the woman can enjoy the husband's success all her life.

Face — Round faces usually mean better luck generally.

Chin — Round fleshy chin or slightly bulging chin means good luck in the late years and good relationship with sons and daughters.

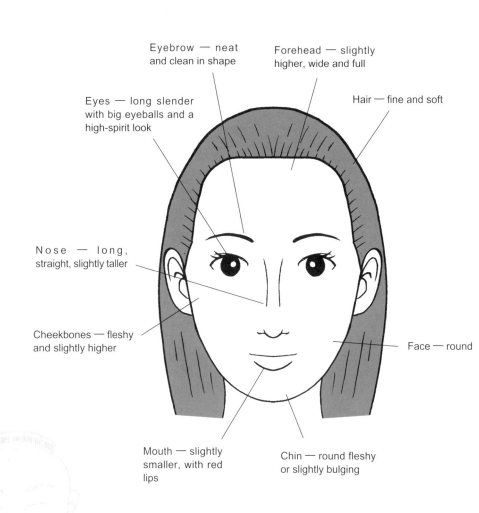

Eyebrow — neat and clean in shape

Forehead — slightly higher, wide and full

Eyes — long slender with big eyeballs and a high-spirit look

Hair — fine and soft

Nose — long, straight, slightly taller

Cheekbones — fleshy and slightly higher

Face — round

Mouth — slightly smaller, with red lips

Chin — round fleshy or slightly bulging

Features that enhances luck of the husband and benefits the woman at the same time

5. A woman who enhances husband's luck without benefiting from husband's success

As opposed to the previous essay, such woman always works hard and handles daily routines for her husband. She has to work harder than those mentioned in the previous category. Therefore, most of such women are more capable but they cannot enjoy a leisurely life as much before they have to make all the decisions for their husbands to have success.

Face — Round and chubby face implies good communications with people and accommodating others' comments. She will get help from people with authority.

Forehead — Such woman has bumpy forehead corners and low hairline. Her eyebrows grow quite far apart and her Xin Tang is full and flat. All these mean she only has normal intelligence but has stamina to hang in there in the times of difficulties. She is also generous, open-minded and does not linger on little details.

Nose — She has a low nose-bridge but high fleshy cheekbones. Low nose-bridge means she cannot sit there and enjoy her husband's success. Here high fleshy cheekbones mean she can help her husband without taking over all her husband's authority.

Mouth — She has a big mouth and thick lips. Thick lips mean she cherishes relationship while being careful on words and that she has the luck to enjoy good food. Big mouth means she is daring and adaptive even in unfamiliar environment. She can then help her husband with his career.

Chin — She had a round fleshy chin with wide jawbones. Round fleshy chin means good luck and accumulated wealth in the old ages. Wide jawbones mean stamina and persistence to encounter failure and achieve success.

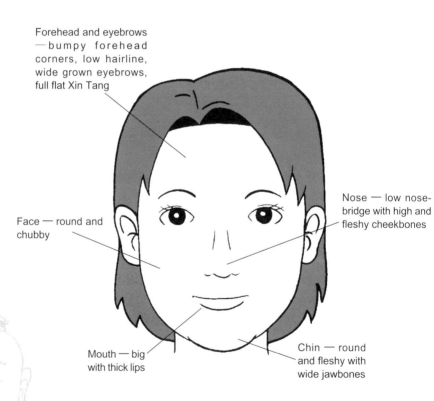

Forehead and eyebrows
— bumpy forehead
corners, low hairline,
wide grown eyebrows,
full flat Xin Tang

Nose — low nose-bridge with high and fleshy cheekbones

Face — round and chubby

Mouth — big with thick lips

Chin — round and fleshy with wide jawbones

Features that enhances the husband's luck without benefiting from his success

6. A person getting good influence on luck from the spouse

Some women are born to just sit back and enjoy their husbands' wealth, while some men always get help from women for success. You can tell by reading their faces.

■ *Women enjoying their husbands' wealth*

With these readings, such women are born to spend their husbands' money and share their husbands' fame.

Straight nose-bridge with high cheekbones — Nose is the location of husband luck on a woman's face. A woman with a tall straight nose bridge usually has a professional husband with much public respect and high social status. In case she also has high fleshy cheekbones, she has excellent marriage luck and her husband is generous. This is a sign of life-long wealth and fame.

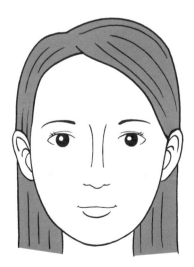

Oval face without protruding cheekbones — Oval face (See Fig 9) is also a sign that the woman can enjoy her husband's success.

In case she also has high fleshy cheekbones, she can actually help her husband and positively influence her husband's luck.

Round fleshy chin — Round fleshy chin (See Fig 10) mean the person is pleasure-type. She can enjoy the benefits from her husbands, sons and daughters. Yet, those who also have a small nose are exceptions as a small nose means poor spousal relationship which cannot be compensated by the good chin.

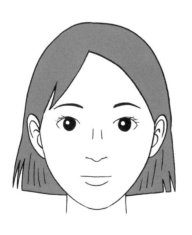

Fig 9   **Fig 10**

Neat eyebrows and clear eyes — Neat eyebrows mean the brow hair is fine and the roots are all visible. The hair is evenly grown and looks continuous. Clear eyes have good definition between the white and the eyeballs. The eyes should have a high-spirit look and should be slightly longer in shape. (See Fig 11) These are signs of wealth and fame. Both she and her husband get famous and high social status easily.

Red lips and white teeth — We always say, "read spirit in men, read health in women." Red lips and white teeth (See Fig 12) mean the woman is healthy with good circulation and these are also signs of highness and wealth. She must marry a husband with fame and social status.

Fig 11

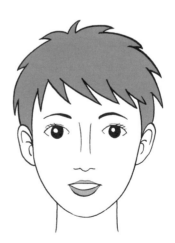

Fig 12

Low nose-bridge with high fleshy cheekbones — Strictly speaking this is not a sign of enjoying the husband's wealth as she has to work hard for her husband to get her share of enjoyment. Yet, if the woman is married to a divorced man, her luck will switch to the relax-and-enjoy category. She does not have to work hard and she will bring luck to her husband. She also has excellent relationship with sons and daughters and a pleasant life in the old ages. (See Fig 13)

A child's nose — It means the nose tip points upward. (See Fig 14) She should not marry a husband of similar age, but should marry someone at least 10 years older. She will then have good marriage luck and her husband will take care of her all her life without any worry.

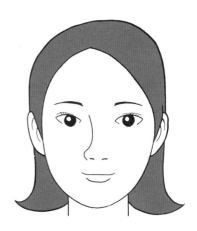

Fig 13   Fig 14

■ *Men getting help from their wives*

These men enjoy the help from their wives on their career all their lives. Whenever there is a problem, their wives will be able to save them.

Thick dense and long eyebrows — Thick and dense eyebrows (See Fig 15) mean the man has good karma with the opposite sex and can get help from females, including his wife. He has especially good development if he works with females.

Round chubby face — A round face (See Fig 16) means the man gets help from powerful or wealthy people and he has good relationship with the opposite sex. In case he also has fleshy cheekbones which are not too low, his wife will help him in his daily routine matters and in his career.

Fig 15

Fig 16

Fleshy chin with high cheekbones — It means good luck in the middle and old ages, good relationship with his wife and offspring. His wife is also a capable person who can enhance his luck. His sons and daughters are respectful and loving. (See Fig 17)

Big tall nose with low cheekbones — As the nose is the location of wife luck on a man's face, a big tall long nose (See Fig 18) means his wife must be capable and virtuous. Yet, such man is stubborn with high self esteem and might be difficult to get along with. He has poor relationship with friends and his offspring. His wife is the only person who supports him and stand by him.

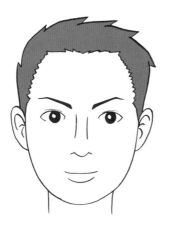

Fig 17   **Fig 18**

7. Features that imply adultery

There are adulterers everywhere. Some of them do it for excitement. Some do it for sexual fulfillment while some do it out of loneliness.

I'll list the facial features of those more likely to engage in adultery. The more such features you have, the higher the chance that you'll engage in adultery.

Thick upper and lower lips — The upper lip represents sentiments while the lower lip represents sexual desire.

People with both lips thick have high sex drives and are very sentimental. (See Fig 19)

Swelling eyelids — The person has strong sexual desire. (See Fig 20)

Fig 19   Fig 20

Long and big nose — The nose represents the penis on a man's face. Long big nose (See Fig 21) means this guy is very enthusiastic about sex.

Curvy eyebrows with fluffy outer end — Curvy eyebrows mean the person is imaginative while fluffy outer end (See Fig 22) means the person is not very smart.

The two traits combine to make such person easily fall in love with people without logical analysis.

Fig 21   **Fig 22**

Long slender tearful eyes — Such person seeks potential dates and sex partners every minute. He/she is promiscuous and likes to play shameful tricks on others to get what he/she needs. (See Fig 23)

Big round eyes — The person is naîve and passionate about love. But he/she mixes up sex and love, which makes him/her engage in adultery easily. (See Fig 24)

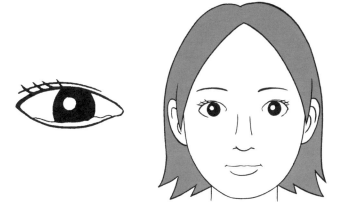

Fig 23   Fig 24

Low nose-bridge ⸺ Women with low nose-bridge (See Fig 25) do not have good marriage luck. But they will meet many married men who show interest in them. They might end up become adulterers.

Big face with a small nose ⸺ Such nose (See Fig 26) is called "mistress nose" as such person is practical and wants to date only those with established career and wealth. Yet, most of these successful people are married. That's why such woman can only be a mistress most of the time.

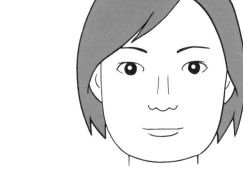

Fig 25   **Fig 26**

Tearful eyes — A woman with such eyes is likely to engage in love triangles. Either she herself or her partner will have an affair outside marriage. (See Fig 27)

Curly hair — It means the person needs sex frequently and cannot tolerate long-term single life without sex. Thus, when his/her spouse or partner travels, loneliness kicks in and such person would have a high risk of being an adulterer. (See Fig 28)

Fig 27   **Fig 28**

Fat and thick base of the palm — The base of the palm is called Mount of Moon, representing imagination. Fat and thick base of the palm, thus, means the person is highly imaginative especially in terms of sexual thoughts. Such palm also implies the person has high sex drive. On top of that, the base of the thumb is called Mount of Venus, representing a person loving character. A fat thick Mount of Venus means the person is very loving and always needs someone by his/her side. He/she cannot tolerate loneliness of living on his/her own.

Thus, full and fleshy Mount of Moon and Mount of Venus work together to make such person needs sex and love both mentally and physically, which might mean he/she has a higher risk of having an affair.

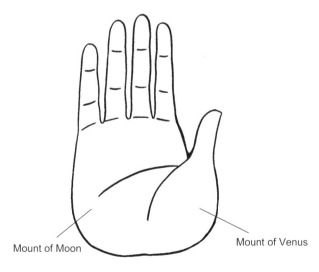

Mount of Moon   Mount of Venus

Line of love affairs under the eye — Such person is susceptible to temptation by the opposite sex all his/her life. (See Fig 29)

Crow feet — Such lines at the outer eye corners (See Fig 30) are signs of poor spousal relationship. The person's wife is either sick all the time or they simply are not passionate about each other. He is unlikely to be with his wife till the end and he is likely to have an affair.

Fig 29   Fig 30

Thick lower lip — It means high sex drive without much reasoning ability. Such person will do anything to gratify his/her sexual needs, including having sex with someone married.

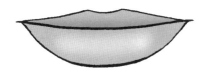

8. Features that imply indiscrimination in love affairs

Such people can be further categorized into "born with love luck", "liars", "true indiscriminate" and "cowardly cheaters."

■ Born with love luck

Such person is not strictly promiscuous as he/she does not actively seek "victims." He/she simply has good luck with the opposite sex who likes and cares for him/her readily. Coupling with his/her sentimental character, he/she simply cannot resist the temptation and becomes indecisive when it comes to love affairs. He/she ends up being annoyed by love all his/her life.

Feature 1: The white of the eye with a pinkish tint

Such eyes imply unwanted or undesirable love relationships. Most of those who have such eyes are men and they are indecisive. No matter how smart and intelligent he is, he simply does not know what to do in front of a woman and he cannot resist any temptation. Particularly from age 35 to 40 (years governed by the eyes), he will experience a very deep and attached relationship. That would be no problem in case he is still single. If he is married, such relationship will ruin his reputation, career and family. (See Fig 31)

Feature 2: Lines of love affairs below the eyes

Such lines mean the person has good karma with the

opposite sex who would love and care for them readily. Such love and care can be converted to relationship easily. (See Fig 32)

Feature 3: Big eyes with big eyeballs

This is also a sign of strong bonds with the opposite sex for both sexes. Such person will meet people who like him or her always. Yet, women with such eyes are unstable in love life. (See Fig 33)

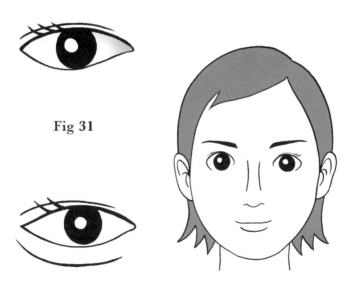

Fig 31

Fig 32

Fig 33

Liars

Such people lie to get what they want. When they win someone's heart, they will find the person is not exactly what they expected. They will just dump that person right away.

Feature 1: Crooked mouth

Whether a person has a crooked mouth (See Fig 34) when he is talking or not, such person has a problem with speech. He/she commits and promises readily without registering. Of course, he/she would make and break the same promise when it comes to relationships.

Feature 2: Disorderly grown teeth or big gap in between front teeth

Such person lies and talks nonsense all the time. To tempt the opposite sex into a relationship, he/she will come up with the sweetest lies. This applies to both sexes. (See Fig 35)

Fig 34   Fig 35

■ *True indiscriminate*

Such person cannot tolerate a long-term monogamous relationship. He/she will fall in love with whoever he/she sees. Such person values novelty and variety over sentiments and love.

Feature 1: Curvy eyebrows with fluffy outer ends

People with curvy eyebrows are imaginative while fluffy outer brow ends mean poor intelligence. (See Fig 36) Such person likes to dream and does not have the ability to analyze. He/she might not be able to bear a life-long relationship with the same person. He/she would feel bored after a while and wants to seek new excitements.

Feature 2: Long slender tearful eyes

Such person is born to be promiscuous and he/she spends all his/her time making connections with the opposite sex. He/she also visits prostitutes or related places frequently. Such person regards sex as a casual act without any spiritual implication. (See Fig 37)

Fig 36   Fig 37

Feature 3: Eyes of ferocity

Ferocious eyes mean the person is ruthless and unattached. He/she treats all kinds of relationships the same way.

Such person will treat the partner only as an object of desire without any sentimental attachment.

Cowardly cheaters

Such person is promiscuous but cowardly at the same time. He is afraid of his wife but sneaks out for potential sex hunt all the same.

Feature 1: Thick dense eyebrows with low-spirit eyes

Thick dense eyebrows mean the person is obsessed with sexual fantasy. Eyes with the low-spirit look mean the person is cowardly. Such person will use his friends as an excuse to meet other women. Yet, he dares not move to the next level for fear that his wife will find out. Such person only dreams without doing much.

9. Features that imply abusive character

Ferocious abusive partners are always sources of stress. Read on for how to avoid such people.

■ Abusive husband

1. Low narrow forehead — Low forehead means the person is stubborn, while narrowness means he lacks analytical power. Needless to say, it is extremely hard to communicate with such person. When poor communication comes in the way, he would opt to resolve with force.

2. Brow bones protruding too much — Such person is short-tempered and cannot control himself.

3. Thick brow hair that sticks out — It means the person is confused in thinking and has low intellectual ability.

4. Ferocious eyes — "Men with ferocious eyes are mostly ruthless," that is how an old saying goes.

5. Cheekbones protruding sideways — He is impulsive and cannot control himself.

6. Angular protruding jawbones — You can see his jawbones sticking out from behind. He is secretive and revengeful.

7. Particularly big and thick thumb — He has an abusive tendency.

8. Particularly short fingers — He is short-tempered and not intelligent. He acts on sudden impulses as his mind simply cannot control his behaviour.

9. Small eyeballs — The smaller the eyeballs, the more ruthless and unattached the person is.

10. Thin lips — It means little sentimental attachment. When the love is gone, he would do anything to release his anger.

Those with the above mentioned traits are likely to abuse their wives.

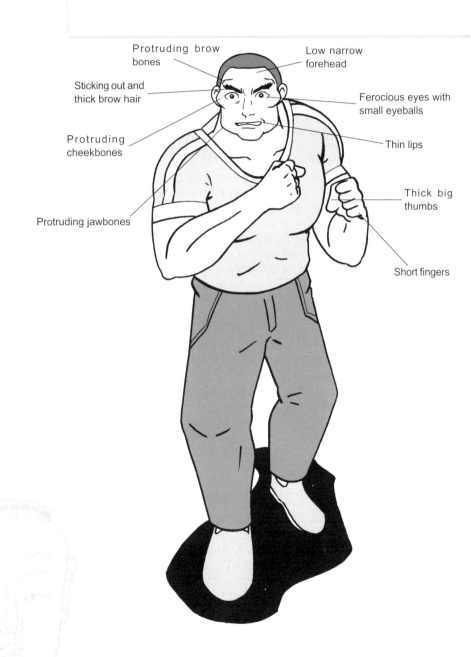

Abusive wife

They share most of the readings of abusive husbands.

1. Curly dry yellow tough hair — The person is stubborn and without much common sense. She also feel she is being treated unfairly.

2. High and protruding forehead — This is a sign of poor luck of marriage for women. She does not have good relationship with her husband.

3. Protruding cheekbones — She has masculine predispositions and likes to fight with her husband.

4. Ferocious eyes — She is revengeful and sentimentally unattached.

5. Particularly small eyeballs — These are also known as "4-white" eyes, i.e. there is white on all sides of the eyeball when she looks normal. Such person is revengeful, ruthless and evil.

6. Small eyes — She hides everything to herself and when she cannot tolerate anymore, she will have a tantrum outburst. She will also take revenge on everything she was not happy about.

7. Bumpy nose-bridge — She is short-tempered and impulses. She is likely to have major problems with relationship

61

at age 20, 29, 38, 41 and 44. She cannot control her thoughts when there is a problem.

8. Protruding brow bones with little brow hair — Protruding brow bones mean the person is impulsive while little brow hair means the person is ruthless.

9. Jawbones protruding sideways — She is secretive, revengeful and destructive in character.

10. Big thick thumbs — She has an abusive tendency.

11. Short fingers — She is short-tempered and her mind cannot control her actions.

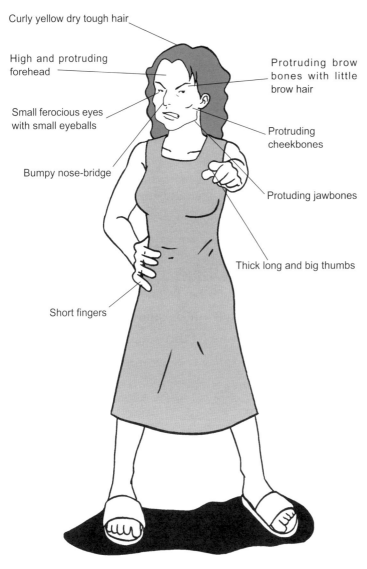

Curly yellow dry tough hair

High and protruding forehead

Protruding brow bones with little brow hair

Small ferocious eyes with small eyeballs

Protruding cheekbones

Bumpy nose-bridge

Protuding jawbones

Thick long and big thumbs

Short fingers

10. Made for each other

Most people think wife and husband with similar facial features are born for each other.

Yet, this is not true.

Wife and husband with same traits and characters are hard to get along as they insist on the same things. Conflicts are especially common when both of them do not yield on all issues.

For instance, if both wife and husband have tall nose-bridge, it means they are both stubborn and with strong self esteem. They will not give up in times of argument and conflicts are likely to happen.

Thus, people with similar facial features are better off being friends as they truly understand each other. Wife and husband truly made for each other should be complementary in characters.

■ *Compatible facial features*

1. Tall nose-bridge with low nose-bridge ― Tall nose-bridge tells a person's high self esteem, subjectivity, uncompromising character and sometimes, poor interpersonal skills. Low nose-bridge implies poor self confidence, lack of subjective views, but also means acceptance of others' comments and good human relationships. Thus, the two come together to reduce to chance of arguments as the side with low nose-bridge would not insist and would yield to the other side. There would be a better chance that the marriage will work out.

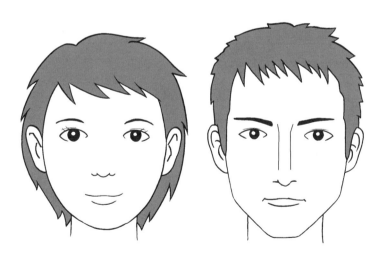

2. Tall and skinny with short and chubby — Most tall skinny people would choose someone short and chubby because of desirability of the "otherness." Just like Asian people want to have the natural curly hair of Caucasians when Caucasians want the straight fine hair of Asians. This is simply a psychological compensation to the lack.

Sometimes, tall skinny people get hooked up with tall skinny people and make good couples. This is said to be "two of a kind" and sometimes it works out too. Yet, a tall skinny person and a regular-build person usually would not work out (same for a short chubby person with a regular-build person) as one of them would tend to think the other is not matching him/herself.

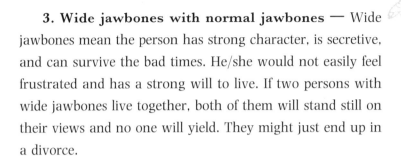

3. Wide jawbones with normal jawbones — Wide jawbones mean the person has strong character, is secretive, and can survive the bad times. He/she would not easily feel frustrated and has a strong will to live. If two persons with wide jawbones live together, both of them will stand still on their views and no one will yield. They might just end up in a divorce.

In case a man with wide jawbone marries a woman with woman with normal jawbones, everything will resolve according to the husband's view.

Similarly, a woman with wide jawbone will make most of the decisions if she gets married to a man with normal jawbone.

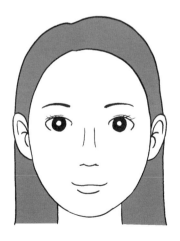

4. Child's nose with older husband — A woman with low nose-bridge and a nose tip that points upwards is said to have a child's nose. Such woman is naïve and innocent. She asks questions always and if she gets married to someone about the same age, her husband will get tired of her and they are unlikely to have a life-long marriage. Yet, in case she gets married with someone at least 10 years older than herself, her husband would be pleased to answer her every question thoughtfully and would take good care of her.

Older men are also interested in such women because of the sense of liveliness and youth they bring. Thus, women with child's nose make perfect match with older men.

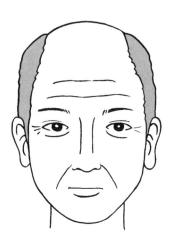

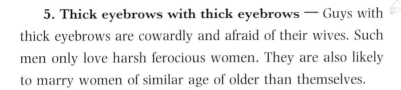

5. Thick eyebrows with thick eyebrows — Guys with thick eyebrows are cowardly and afraid of their wives. Such men only love harsh ferocious women. They are also likely to marry women of similar age of older than themselves.

Women with thick eyebrows have masculine predispositions. They like socializing and lead lives independent of their husbands. Such women usually meet younger guys who listen to whatever they say.

Thus, a man and a woman with thick eyebrows make perfect match.

6. Big mouth with small mouth — People with big mouths are daring while people with small mouth are cowardly.

Those with big mouths take initiative and are not shy to make new friends in an unfamiliar environment. Those with small mouths do not adapt to new environments very well and they are passive all the time. They also keep things to themselves and are narrow-minded. Thus, the active character of a person with big mouth matches the passive character of a person with small mouth perfectly.

7. Low hair line with older husband — A woman with low hairline does not have good relationship with her father.

As she lacks the fatherly love since childhood, she is likely to pick a lover who also doubles as father figure. If she marries someone just a few years older, she would not think he is caring enough. If she marries a man at least 10 years older than herself, her husband is a lot more tolerant and they can enjoy a happy marriage.

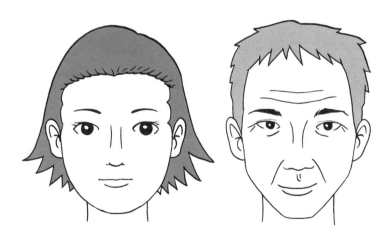

8. Small nose with someone married — A woman whose nose is disproportionally small when compared with the face, are likely to be mistress. A small nose means lack of self confidence and the tendency to live on someone with established wealth and career. Yet such successful person is likely to be married. She might as well be his mistress without other choices. Such woman has surprising happy and good relationship being a mistress. Yet, if she is married as a regular wife, she has bad marriage luck and her husband will suffer from bad luck. They would end up in a divorce.

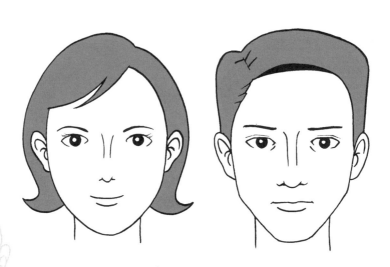

11. Those who adversely influence the spouses' luck

■ *A man who adversely influences his wife's luck:*

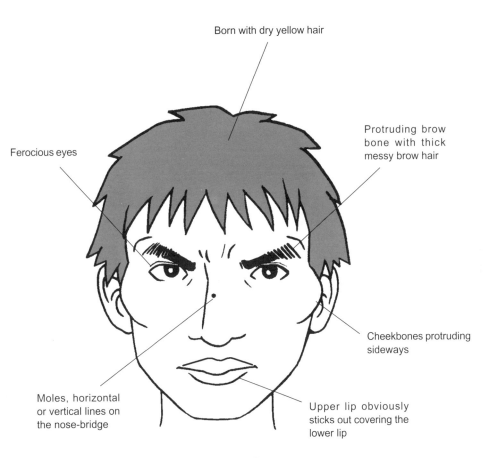

Born with dry yellow hair

Protruding brow bone with thick messy brow hair

Ferocious eyes

Cheekbones protruding sideways

Moles, horizontal or vertical lines on the nose-bridge

Upper lip obviously sticks out covering the lower lip

■ *A woman who adversely influences her husband's luck:*

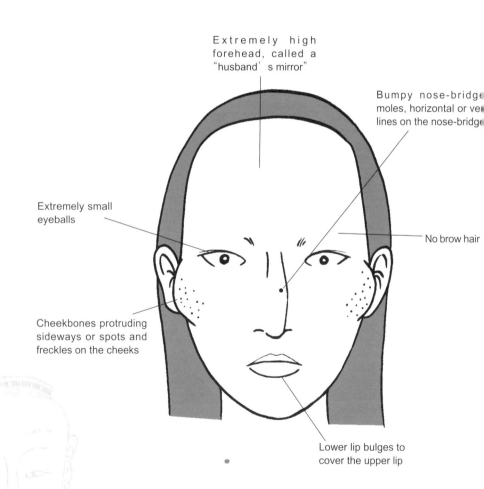

Extremely high forehead, called a "husband's mirror"

Bumpy nose-bridge, moles, horizontal or ver... lines on the nose-bridge

Extremely small eyeballs

No brow hair

Cheekbones protruding sideways or spots and freckles on the cheeks

Lower lip bulges to cover the upper lip

Anyone with 3 of those readings are considered adversely affecting the spouse's luck and they are much better off marrying "not-so-regular" partners.

A man with such readings should marry a woman 10 years older or younger than himself; or marry someone abroad, or a divorced or widowed woman. Then the bad luck will be resolved.

A woman with 3 of those readings should marry a man at least 10 years older than herself, someone of the same age or younger than herself, or a divorced man, or a man abroad.

Section 2

Wealth and Career

12. What job is the best for you?

The Five Elements in Chinese belief are Metal, Wood, Water, Fire and Earth. People are classified into these 5 main categories, each of which has specific attributes that make them suitable for a certain type of jobs. Someone who has a job that fits his/her element type will of course have achievements more easily. Someone who has an incompatible job has to work a lot harder to achieve the same.

■ Metal

Features — They have a square face and wide jawbones. Those who have pale complexion are true Metal-type while those with a dark complexion are Metal-type with Water influences.

Best jobs — They have the best development working in areas like professional sports and martial arts, or they might work in the army, police force or any other jobs that demand risk-taking. Labourers also have such face. If they get the right job, they will have success. Otherwise, they will just work hard all their lives without much pay-off.

Good signs — Protruding brow bones, thick eyebrows and eyes with a strong look are good signs that the person will enjoy success from the youth ages (age 30 to 40).

A tall straight nose-bridge or a bumpy nose-bridge with obvious cheekbones are signs of success in the middle ages

(age 40 to 50).

Bad signs — Protruding brow bones but messy brow hair and eyes with a low-spirit look, or bloodshot eyes are bad signs. Besides, crooked or tall bony nose; protruding bony cheekbones are signs that the person will not have major achievements. He/she is likely to work all his/her life without a break.

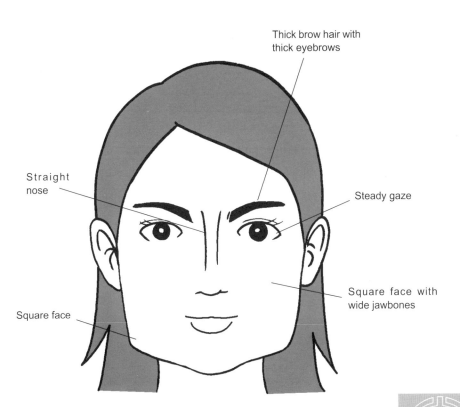

Thick brow hair with thick eyebrows

Straight nose

Steady gaze

Square face with wide jawbones

Square face

■ *Wood*

Features — They have long skinny face or their foreheads are wide and their chins are pointy. They have pale complexion with a green tint. They have wide shoulders and tall skinny build.

Best jobs — They work best in office jobs that need thinking, say, creative director, writer, lawyer, literature writer, inventor, philosopher, professor or secretary.

Good signs — Neatly grown eyebrows with thin brow hair, big eyeballs with a strong look are signs that the person will stand out among others before the age of 30.

An ancient face-reading document says, "All young successful officers have pale green faces (i.e. Wood-type face)." Those with long straight nose will get wealthy in the middle ages.

Bad signs — Wide forehead and pointy chin, but eyes with a low-spirit look and small nose are signs that the person thinks too much without action. He/she is likely to waste all his/her life complaining not having the right opportunities.

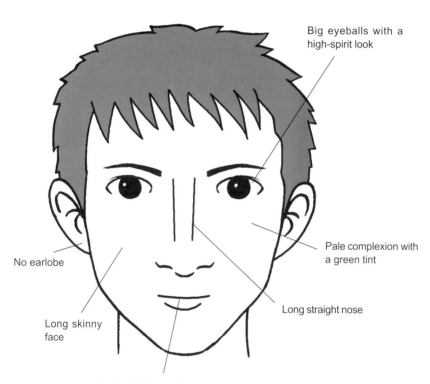

Big eyeballs with a high-spirit look

Pale complexion with a green tint

No earlobe

Long straight nose

Long skinny face

Mouth slightly smaller than normal

■ *Water*

Features — They have round face, thick but short eyebrows, round eyes, round nose, thick lips and a wide chin. Those who have dark complexion are true Water-type while those with pale complexion are Water-type with Metal influences.

Best jobs — They have the best development in jobs involving socializing with people, such as public relations, politics, comedy acting or starting their own business.

Good signs — Thin brow hair showing every root clearly, round eyes with a strong look and big eyeballs, small and short nose with low nose-bridge, thick red lips and double chin are good signs that the person will have a stable luck without any major frustration.

He/she is also highly skilful in interpersonal relationship and does not have many enemies in his/her life.

Bad signs — Messy brow hair, glossy eyes and crooked mouth are signs that the person cannot be someone important. His/her luck is so-so without any achievement. Yet, he/she would have no problem having enough money for basic needs.

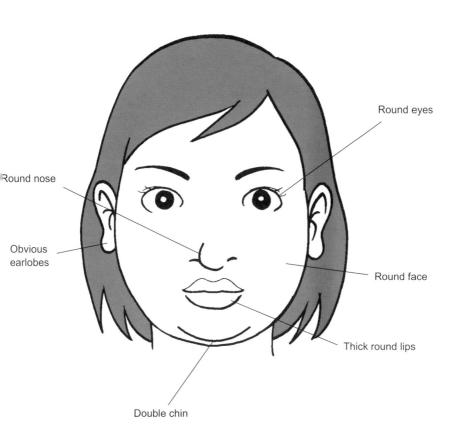

Round eyes

Round nose

Obvious
earlobes

Round face

Thick round lips

Double chin

■ *Fire*

Features — They have a face like an upright triangle (i.e. narrow at the top, wider at the bottom) and a strong build no matter they are chubby or skinny. They also have pinkish complexion.

Best jobs — They work best in the army and police force, or as expedition experts, explosive experts or anything with a destructive nature.

Good signs — Protruding brow bones, neatly grown eyebrows with thick brow hair, eyes with a strong look, some capillaries in the white of the eyes, long straight nose or bumpy nose, obvious cheekbones, tightly closed mouth with thin lips are all good signs.

The major good features are wide jawbones. Such person has stamina to deal with difficulties and achieve success.

Bad signs — Protruding brow bones with little or no brow hair mean the person is ruthless and do not know when to do the right thing. Those with ferocious eyes, crooked tall bony nose-bridge and thick lips are always involved in gang fights and violent crime. They lack patience and they are unlikely to succeed.

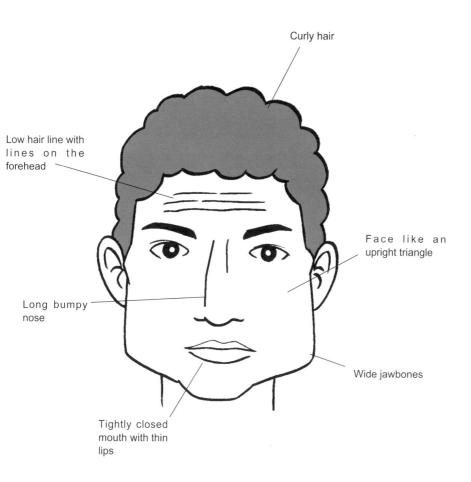

Curly hair

Low hair line with lines on the forehead

Face like an upright triangle

Long bumpy nose

Wide jawbones

Tightly closed mouth with thin lips

■ *Earth*

Features — They have short wide face with round outline and firm flesh. Their complexion is earthy yellow and they have thick back muscles.

They walk slowly and they are highly credible. They also have thick lips, thick eyebrows but sparsely grown thin brow hair.

Best jobs — They have the best development in business.

Good signs — Gentle and peaceful gaze, fleshy nose, wide fleshy face and a double or wide chin are good signs.

Among the Five Elements, the Earth-type has the highest potential to be wealthy. People with Earth-type face usually have high social status and good smooth luck all their lives.

Bad signs — Unsteady gaze, crooked nose, thin lips and talkative, bony or skinny face are all signs that the person can only make enough money for basic needs.

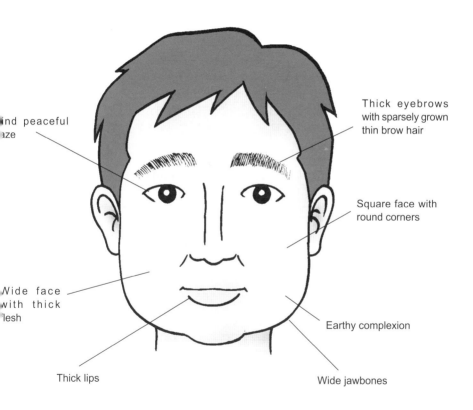

...nd peaceful
...aze

Thick eyebrows
with sparsely grown
thin brow hair

Square face with
round corners

Wide face
with thick
flesh

Earthy complexion

Thick lips

Wide jawbones

13. Luck of unstable income

Some guys have all the luck. Some people win the jackpots in the lottery a few times in a row while some of us never even get a small prize in lucky draws. There are certain facial and palm features that tell a certain person has luck of unstable income. The more of such features you have, the higher the chance you can get unstable income.

▪ *Features of good luck of unstable income*

1. Fleshy cheekbones — Those with fleshy cheekbones always have help from powerful people or others bring them good luck. Such people should ask a third person to buy lottery tickets for a better chance to win.

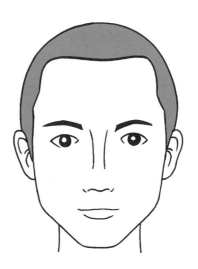

2. Thin nose wings — Nose tip governs stable income while nose wings govern unstable income. Thin nose wings mean the person has fluent cashflow and has a good luck of unstable income. (See Fig 38)

3. Long straight tall nose — This is a sign of wealth. The person works close to powerful people and others also bring him good luck and give him help. Supervisors will take care of him/her and they have a much better chance to make extra money. (See Fig 39)

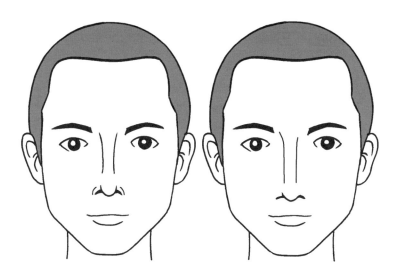

Fig **38**   Fig **39**

4. Pointy nose tip — Nose tip governs stable income and a big nose tip suppresses the luck of unstable income. On the other hand, a pointy nose means the person gets unstable income easily. Yet, his/her nose should be long and straight to enjoy that luck as there are not many wealthy people with short nose (except women). (See Fig 40)

5. Normal nose shape — As the nose is the location of wealth, even though a normal nose does not mean particular good luck of unstable income, the person might have good general luck at one point of his life that might bring some extra money.

6. Line of wealth under the ring finger — From palm reading point of view, a clear straight line of wealth right under the ring finger means the person has good luck of wealth. Such line would help luck of wealth no matter it is stable or unstable. (See Fig 41)

7. Line of unstable wealth — It is similar to the line of wealth, but it starts at the edge of the palm and goes all the way to the base of the ring finger. Such person makes extra money all the time. (See Fig 42)

8. Asterisk under the ring finger — Asterisk means short-term glamour and the person makes lucky money. Even though he/she might just spend it right away, he/she can still make it again. (See Fig 43)

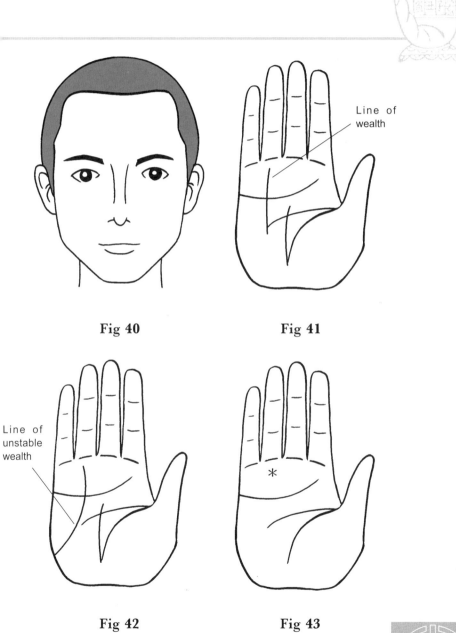

Fig 40

Line of wealth

Fig 41

Line of unstable wealth

Fig 42

*

Fig 43

9. Long ring finger with a line of intelligence pointing downward — Long ring finger implies the person likes to take risk. A line of intelligence pointing downward means the person likes to dream. Such combination gives rise to the mentality of either a fine artist or professional gambler. In case he/she also has a line of wealth, he/she is likely to make unstable money.

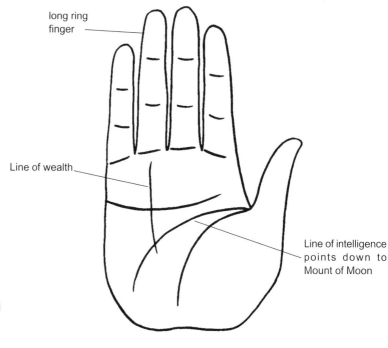

long ring finger

Line of wealth

Line of intelligence points down to Mount of Moon

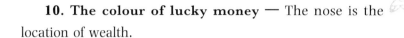

10. The colour of lucky money ― The nose is the location of wealth.

If there is a patch of white colour goes all the way from the nose to the Xin Tang, the person will make lucky money shortly.

11. Centre of the palm is white in colour ― White complexion of the palm means the person does not have to work hard for money. The person just sits there and money comes to him/her. He/she also makes lucky money.

■ *Features of poor luck of unstable income*

1. Pointy bony cheekbones ⎯ Cheekbones govern the enhancement of luck by others. Bony pointy cheekbones (See Fig 44) mean the person does not get any help from others and others do not bring good luck. Thus, he/she should always buy lottery tickets himself.

2. Especially big nose ⎯ Big nose (See Fig 45) suppresses the luck of unstable income and implies the person only makes money the conventional steady way. He/she has to work hard for the money and has to do everything on his/her own.

Fig 44   Fig 45

3. Big round overhanging nose tip — Such is also a sign of stable income. The person only believes in making money with careful calculation and thoughtful set up. He/she does not believe in unstable income.

4. Red palm — Such is a sign of hard money as the person has to work hard by him/herself to make every dime. He/she is destined to make money after lots of work and will not make lucky money.

5. Yellow palm — Such is a sign of poor luck of wealth, no matter it is stable or unstable. As yellow palm is the colour of unfruitful hard work, the person will not have lucky money.

■ *Features that imply loss of money*

1. Acnes on the nose tip — Nose tip governs the luck of stable income. Acnes on the nose tip means the person will lose his/her stable income. If he/she gambles at that moment, he/she will just lose it.

2. Acnes on the nose wings — That means the person will lose his/her unstable income. For instance, if he/she gambles he/she will lose all the money and borrow a loan from someone. The person will lose more than he/she can afford.

3. Imbalance between the left and right nose wings (in terms of position and size) — Such nose means the person must lose every time he/she gambles. He/she will never make lucky money and should refrain from gambling altogether. (See Fig 46)

4. Long ring finger with a line of intelligence pointing downward, but without a line of wealth — Such person takes risk and loves to fantasize, but without any luck. He/she will lose most of the time. (See Fig 47)

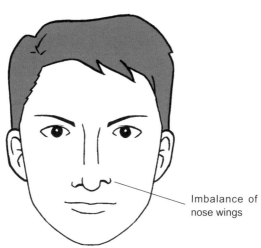

Imbalance of
nose wings

Fig 46

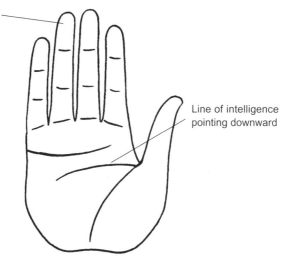

Long ring finger

Line of intelligence
pointing downward

Fig 47

14. Read your boss' characters

Intensive sucking-up works for some but absolutely annoys many. Some bosses simply don't want to be flattered. Before you use any of your old tricks, read your boss' character first.

■ *Those who like to be flattered (See Fig 48)*

1. Short philtrum (the groove between the nose and the mouth) — It means the person loves to be flattered and those who offer more praises and please him/her more get promoted more quickly.

2. Round face — It means the person loves to be accompanied at all time to highlight his/her own presence as a superior. Such person cares so much about the "look" and will take as much flattering words as you can offer.

3. Low nose-bridge — The person has low self-esteem and loves to listen to gossips. It works great if you can find someone with the small temperament to offer him/her some pleasing words.

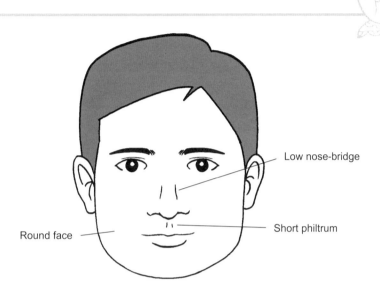

Low nose-bridge

Short philtrum

Round face

Fig 48: Boss who likes to be flattered

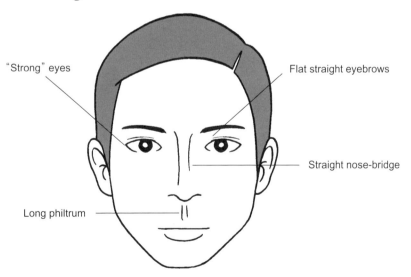

"Strong" eyes

Flat straight eyebrows

Straight nose-bridge

Long philtrum

Fig 49: Boss who don't like to be flattered

■ *Those who don't like to be flattered (See Fig 49)*

1. Long philtrum — Such person is suspicious and incredulous. Even if you flatter him/her with the most wonderful words in the world, he/she would simply suspect your intention. So save your tricks on such bosses.

2. "Strong" eyes — Eyes with a "strong" or high-spirit look mean the person has strong analytical power and such boss knows well in his/her heart which employee has good performance. Pleasing him/her with excessive words is not going to change his/her mind.

3. Straight nose-bridge — It means strong confidence and the person believes only in what he/she sees or knows. Again, taking him/her into believing your capability when you don't show any is not going to work.

4. Flat straight eyebrows — The person has a strong sense of justice and he/she knows who has done what. If you haven't done anything and simply want such boss to take you under his/her wings by sucking up, you are destined to fail.

Besides reading if your boss loves flattering or not, you can also tell whether your boss is generous or miserly. Next time when you go for a job interview, pick a boss who wouldn't squeeze every buck out of you.

■ *Generous boss*

1. Pointy bony nose — The person has the temper of an artist and is a perfectionist.

2. Nose wings showing the nostrils — The person is born to have luck of unstable income. He/she makes money and spends money freely. Such person will treat the employees right when he/she makes money.

3. Depressed temples — Such person does not care about money too much. He/she will pay you as much as you ask if you are worth it.

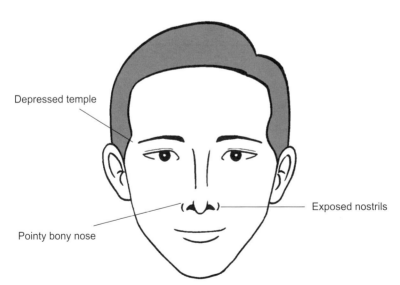

Depressed temple

Exposed nostrils

Pointy bony nose

■ *Miserly boss*

1. Full temples — Such person has a habit of saving money. He/she is a miser no matter how much money he/she has saved.

2. Small nostrils — The nostrils are like the doors of a safe. The smaller the nostrils, the more money a person can save. You don't need me to tell you it's hard to bargain for a raise in salary with such boss.

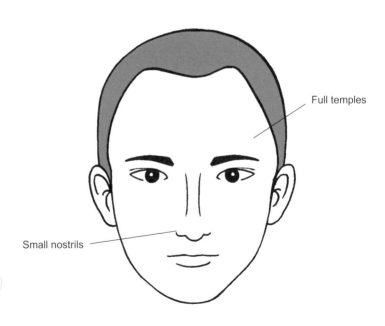

Full temples

Small nostrils

15. Read your subordinates' characters

How do you tell the loyal people from traitors among a whole lot of applicants for a job? How do you know which person is a great business partner among all your acquaintances? Read their faces!

■ *Traitors (See Fig 50)*

Low nose-bridge — It means the person is selfish and material-oriented. He/she will shift to where the money is and will sell out others in return for his/her own benefits.

Crooked nose — Such person is evil at heart and get his/her employer and friends into troubles.

Unsteady gaze — The person does not have the potential to be in the upper management but he/she is good at playing politics. He/she appears to do according to what the boss says but he/she breaks all the rules behind the boss' back.

Jawbones protruding too much — Such person is a natural born destroyer. He/she breaks the old system down to build one that he/she can manipulate.

■ *Loyalists (See Fig 51)*

Straight balanced nose ▔ It means the person thinks straight without much evil thinking. A nose of moderate size means he/she will not overwhelm the boss' authority. Such person is a highly reliable employee.

Low-spirit look ▔ The person is not very daring. Even if another employer offers something better, he/she dare not take the risk to quit.

Good mouth ▔ A balanced mouth without flaws like moles, lines or scars is considered good. Such person takes responsibility and cares about credibility.

Neatly grown teeth ▔ The person can keep secrets.

Long eyebrows with brow hair growing close to the skin and a wide Xin Tang ▔ The person is optimistic and will think positively even when the company faces difficulties. He/she will not switch jobs casually.

Fig 50: Traitor

Fig 51: Loyalist

Fig 52: Capable employee

Fig 53: Financial controller

There are two more types of faces that are more likely to earn a boss' appreciation:

■ *Capable employees (See Fig 52)*

High nose-bridge — It means the person has strong confidence and cares about fame and social status.

He/she is management grade material.

"Strong" eyes — Or a high-spirit look in the eyes means the person is decisive and smart. He/she is also healthy and strong.

Balanced mouth — The person cares about credibility and will not make casual promises or say things he/she doesn't mean.

Square face — The person has stamina and will not give up half way through a project.

▉ *Financial controllers (See Fig 53)*

Big nose — Nose is considered the location of wealth and a person with big nose can manage big sum of money.

Straight nose-bridge — It means strong self esteem. In case the person also has "strong" eyes, he/she will never cheat to make improper money from the employer.

Wide chin — The chin tells how capable a person is in terms of handling subordinates. A wide chin means his/her subordinates are obedient and he/she leads a stable life. When a person can live well, he/she is less likely to commit any improper deals.

Neat brow ends — It means the person is not involved in gambling and risky investment activities. He/she is conservative in terms of handling money.

Such person gives the boss much confidence when he/she is hired as a financial controller.

◼ Resolving poor employer-employee relationship

What if I was born with a nasty face? Of course, you should work hard and do your own job first. Then you can also use a few Feng Shui tricks to resolve the bad luck and improve your boss' impression on you.

If both you and your boss were born between 6th May and 8th August (i.e. both of you have a "hot" predisposition), put a glass of water on your table.

If both of you were born between 9th August and 6th March (i.e. both of you have a "cold" predisposition), decorate your desk with a lamp or some red accessories.

If one of you has "hot" while the other has "cold" predisposition, put a plant on your desk.

Those born between 6th March and 6th May have "neutral" predisposition and they would not have any problem with employer-employee relationship.

16. The ups and downs of life

Everybody has a brilliant moment in his or her life.

We would not regret it as long as we seize the moment and do as much as we can. It is important to locate that certain peak of luck. Some of us had passed that point without knowing it while some would have their best luck in their elderly years.

Read this article carefully to find out which years are the highlights of your life. (The calculation of ages in this article is according to a special method of luck for individual years.)

■ *Early youth ages*

Good luck — The forehead tells the luck from age 16 to 26. High, wide and full forehead with a shiny bright colour without any flaws like moles, lines or scars means the person has a surprisingly successful career before the age of 26 and he/she should take advantage of his/her good luck then.

High, wide and
full forehead

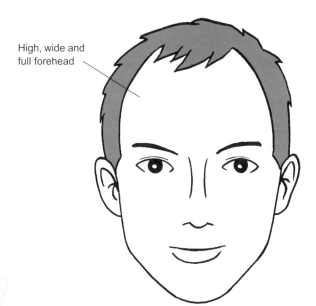

Bad luck — A narrow forehead with low hair line and dry tough hair means the person has poor luck in the early youth ages.

The person should get better education and training so that he/she can have good development when the good luck kicks in later in his/her life.

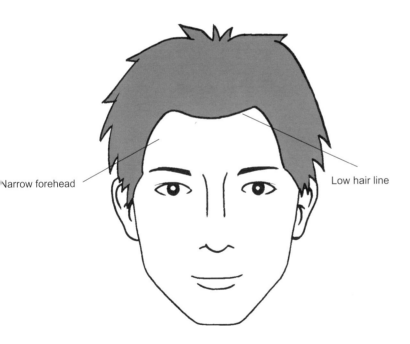

Narrow forehead

Low hair line

■ *Middle youth ages*

Good luck — The eyebrows govern the luck from age 26 to 36. Those having long flat eyebrows with fine brow hair showing every root clearly and growing close to the brow bones have good luck in this period.

They enjoy much help from friends and people of the same rank and have a good start to their career making major progress soon afterwards. Therefore, they should seize the opportunities between the age of 26 and 36.

Bad luck — Those who have thick eyebrows with disorderly grown and fluffy brow hair or those with brow hair sticking out and brow hair grown in a crisscross pattern have poor luck associated with friends and siblings.

They have poor interpersonal relationship, might get involved in court cases and gang fights from age 26 to 36. Those having such eyebrows should donate blood often in those years to resolve the bad luck. Also refrain from any form of investment in those years, including investment with someone else.

■ Late youth ages

Good luck — The eyes govern the luck from age 36 to 46.

People having big eyeballs with clear definition between the white and the iris and a high-spirit "strong" look in the eyes have their peak of luck in those 10 years. They should make good use of every opportunity in those years for a successful career.

Bad luck — Those who have eyes that look like drunken or sleepy or look "weak" and low-spirit have poor luck in between age 36 and 46.

They should then hang in there and should not act out of impulses. They can wait till better luck comes or else they would work hard without any pay-off or even suffer from major disasters.

■ *Middle ages*

Good luck — The nose governs luck from age 46 to 56. A long straight nose-bridge that is tall and free of bumps, coupling with fleshy cheekbones means the person gets help from others to enhance his luck.

Such nose implies he/she will meet people with authority who will give him/her major achievements in terms of social status in those years and this is especially true for politicians.

Bad luck — A small nose with a low nose bridge, a nose-tip without fullness or a firm outline and low depressed cheekbones means poor luck from age 36 to 46.

Such person should just hang in there in those years and refrain from acting out of impulses. He/she will suffer from major loss otherwise.

Elderly ages

Good luck — The mouth governs luck from age 56 to 66. A good mouth should be balanced in shape, with bright red upper and lower lips of equal and appropriate thickness. Fullness around the philtrum and a wide chin also contribute the luck in these years. Having good mouth luck means peaceful and pleasant old ages with many servants to order around and loving caring sons and daughters. Such person also has accumulated substantial amount of wealth by this time.

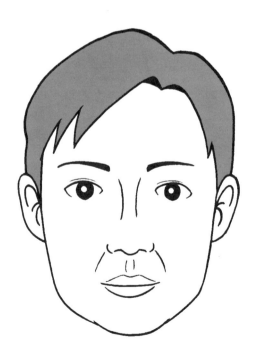

Bad luck — On the other hand, those who do not have fullness around the philtrum, crooked mouth, thin lips that are dark green in colour and a point bony chin have poor luck in those years.

They should aim at maintaining what they have in those years and do not act aggressively to expand their business or their wealth. They can then have a peaceful life in their final years and not ending up losing everything.

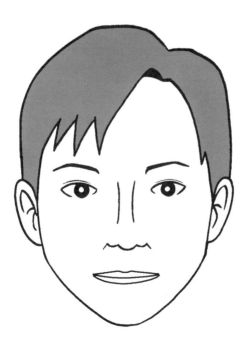

119

17. Features of movie stars

Some of us get treated like movie stars all the time as people tend to be nice and welcoming all the time. Actually, there are certain facial features that make them so popular. Here are such features for males and females:

▇ *Male*

Rectangular forehead means the person is practical and his/her action is in line with his/her thoughts. Such person gets respect from people easily.

Neatly grown brow hair and eyebrows slightly thicker than normal mean the person is decisive and efficient.

Long eyes of hig spirit with clea definition between th whites and the iris and big eyeballs th look sad mean th person is very lovabl

Long straight nose means the person is masculine and manly.

Mouth corners curving upward like a new moon give a sense of closeness and friendliness.

An obvious line in the cheek when smiling means the person have excellen relationship with people and good karma even with strangers.

Female

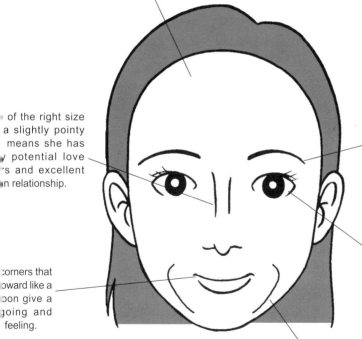

Round high and full forehead that is a little big when compared with the size of her face mean she has good youth luck and gets recognition early.

Long curvy eyebrows with neatly grown brow hair mean the person has an aesthetic mind and artistic talent that wins others' liking.

of the right size a slightly pointy means she has potential love s and excellent n relationship.

Big eyes with big eyeballs are called child's eyes. She is innocent in thinking and loves to ask questions all the time. Others think she is cute and lovely.

corners that oward like a oon give a joing and feeling.

An obvious line on the cheek when smiling means she has excellent interpersonal relationship and good karma even with strangers.

18. Features that imply successful career

A proverb has it that "men stand up at an age of 30," which means men starts to have a change of luck and turn from an anonymous kid into a successful entrepreneur at age 30. Besides luck and ability, their face also contributes to their career.

A good forehead — It is the reading point for intelligence, youth luck, help from others and career. A good forehead should be high, full and free from any flaws like lines, moles and scars. It means the person has good luck in his youth ages and he/she is likely to be the second generation of wealthy family. On the contrary, the first generation millionaires who earn the first bucket of gold out of nothing usually have bad foreheads.

Good eyebrows — Usually the first generation millionaires have messy fluffy brow hair. The second generation who enjoys the fortune from parents has much neater eyebrows. Those who have outer brow ends pointing upward usually have high social status and are not comfortable being subordinate to others.

"Strong" eyes — Eyes with a high-spirit look gives an impression of strong confidence. "Strong" eyes also make things work smoother naturally. Of course, the clear definition between the whites and the irises is also important.

Tall nose-bridge — Those with tall nose-bridge usually

hold important positions in society and they have respectable social status. A long nose means the person has an elegant character. Therefore people with successful career usually have long tall nose and not a big nose.

High cheekbones — High cheekbones (in terms of position, not in terms of degree of protrusion, so these are not protruding bony cheekbones) mean the person has authority and power. Cheekbones should also be read with the nose as high cheekbones with tall nose mean the person has much power and matching social status. High cheekbones with low nose mean the person has power but not the social status, so that he/she will fight with his/her supervisors for power.

Deep obvious philtrum — Read the philtrum for career after the age of 40. Long deep wide and obvious philtrum means the person can hold important position and have a reputation that gets better with time. He/she can also get respect from obedient subordinates.

Full lips — Full and slightly protruding lips mean the person has much wealth and knows how to enjoy life.

A chin that points forward — People with a full chin that points slightly forward have a peaceful and enjoyable life in the old ages. They do not have to worry about money and they have established career by then.

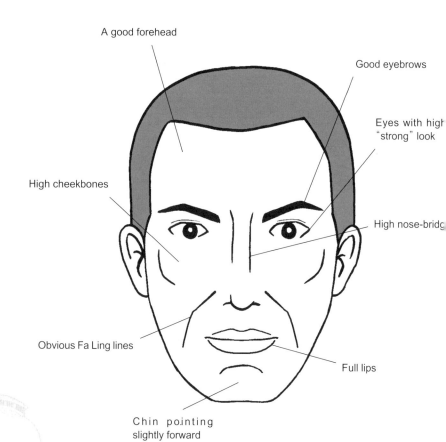

A good forehead

Good eyebrows

Eyes with high "strong" look

High cheekbones

High nose-bridge

Obvious Fa Ling lines

Full lips

Chin pointing slightly forward

19. The palms of the leaders

The Chinese Premier raised his hand and waved at the people in the handover ceremony in 1997. His palm can be clearly seen and let's read the palms of Premier Jiang Xe-min and Hong Kong Chief Executive Tung Chee-hua.

Read characters from the palms

The palm tells a person's personality and ability. The palms of Premier Jiang and Chief Executive Tung are quite different and that means they are quite different in terms of characters.

Always remember to read the left palm before the age of 30 and read the right palm after the age of 30 (the opposite is true for left-handed people). Therefore, I read the right palms of both leaders.

■ *Premier Jiang Xe-min*

1. Square palm — Practical thinking

His palm is square in shape which means he is very capable and practical.

2. White palm — Strong good luck

Light coloured palm means he has excellent luck at that time.

3. Long thumb — Decisiveness

A thumb is considered long if it reaches the midpoint of the third segment of the index finger when the palm is flat. A long thumb means he is decisive and once the decision is made no one can alter his mind.

4. Long index finger — Leadership

An index finger is considered long if it reaches the midpoint of the first segment of the middle finger. A long index finger means the person has authority. The third segment of his index finger is very plump and fleshy which means he has a strong desire to hold power.

5. Line of intelligence separated from the line of health completely — Impulsive character

The line of intelligence separated from the line of health

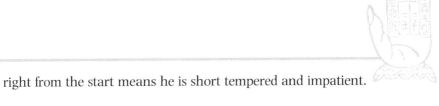

right from the start means he is short tempered and impatient.

6. Line of health extend beyond the middle of the palm — Living away from homeland

A clear and sharp line of health means he is still very healthy. The line also extends beyond the centre of the palm into the left half. It means he might emigrate to a foreign country in his elderly years.

7. Long and curvy line of love relationships

A line of love relationship is considered long if it ends between the base of the index and middle fingers.

Premier Jiang's line of love relationship is long and curving upward which is called "the line of satisfaction in love". He is willing to invest emotionally and is satisfied with his love life.

127

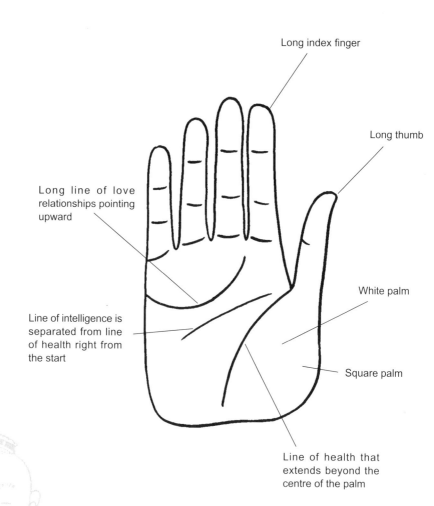

Long index finger

Long thumb

Long line of love
relationships pointing
upward

White palm

Line of intelligence is
separated from line
of health right from
the start

Square palm

Line of health that
extends beyond the
centre of the palm

The palm of Premier Jiang Xe-min

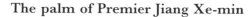

■ *Chief Executive Tung Chee-Hua*

1. Long skinny hand — Thought-type

His fingers are slender and have obvious bulging joints. There are gaps between the fingers even when he forces his fingers together. Such palm is the philosopher's type and he pursues spiritual gratification.

2. Red palm — Hard life

His palm is all red which means he is short-tempered and impulsive. He also has to work hard all his life without much pay-off.

3. Short thumb — Indecisive character

His thumb is not long enough which means he gets influenced by others easily and he is not decisive.

4. Long small finger — Strong planning ability

A small finger is considered long if it passes the first joint of the ring finger. It means he has a scientific mind (In fact, he has a Bachelor of Science degree from the University of Liverpool).

He also knows how to delegate the right jobs to the right persons. Yet, combined with his indecisiveness, all those marvelous plans he has might not be realized at all.

5. Line of intelligence pointing downward — Empty dreamer

His line of intelligence goes all the way to the Mount of Moon which means he is full of imagination. This combined with his "philosopher's palm" retards his philosophical ability and makes his thoughts too idealistic.

6. Line of longevity splits into two — Living away from homeland

There is an obvious branch to his line of health which is called "emigration line". Tung will move out of Hong Kong.

■ *The luck of Hong Kong is not related to the luck of the leaders*

Even though the head of Hong Kong will switch after the handover, from the strict point of view of Feng Shui, the luck of Hong Kong is independent from the leaders. The land luck of Hong Kong runs from 1964 to 2023 so that the development of Hong Kong is still looking good until the year of 2023.

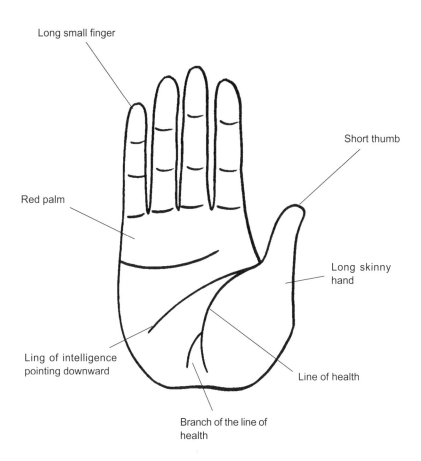

Long small finger

Short thumb

Red palm

Long skinny hand

Ling of intelligence pointing downward

Line of health

Branch of the line of health

The palm of Tung Chee-hua

Section 3

Knowing the Right People

20. Features of a good mother

Being a good mother is of course not an easy task — she has to communicate well with the children; she has to be patient, and she has to be a good role model for children.

Now I'm listing the facial features of a potential good mother so that you can compare with your own.

Forehead — A good mother cannot have a low hairline as those who have low hairline are stubborn and cannot accept the comments from children. They like to impose their own standards and points of view onto the children and never let the children express freely. The children will hence be unable to develop fully to their potential.

Eyebrows — Mothers with thick eyebrows are always careless and thoughtless. They only take care of the big things overlooking all the details. They don't like house chores and cannot take good care of the children.

On the other hand, those with fine eyebrows are thoughtful and observant. They understand the needs of the children and do a good job in housekeeping.

Eyes — They are the windows to the soul and you can read a person's psyche from the eyes. Whether the person is cunning or honest, smart or stupid, virtuous or evil, decisive or hesitant can all be read from the eyes.

Generally speaking, those with big eyeballs are gentle

while those with small eyeballs are ruthless. Clear definition between the whites and the irises means the person is decisive. Eyes with a "weak" or low-spirit look mean the person is indecisive and hesitant.

A gentle gaze means the person is kind at heart while a ferocious gaze means the person does not have sentimental attachment to others. Round and big eyes imply the person expresses his/her feelings well while small eyes mean the person hide everything from others.

Therefore, a good mom should have big eyes, with big eyeballs, clear definition between the whites and the irises and a gentle warm gaze.

Lips — The upper lip refers to love while the lower lip refers to sex. Thick upper and lower lips mean the person cares about relationship and sentiments, including love for the husband or for the children.

Those having both upper and lower lips thin are detached in emotions and keep their feeling to themselves. A mouth with thin upper lip and sparsely grown teeth is not good as thin upper lip means she is talkative while sparsely grown teeth imply she is not articulate about language. Such is the mouth of an irritable mom that nags all the time. The worst mouth is crooked as she is likely to be a habitual liar who can never be a good role model for kids.

Chin ⏤ The chin is the location of family.

A round fleshy chin means the mother put family in a very important position in her heart. On the other hand, a pointy bony chin means she only treats home as a place to sleep.

Therefore, those moms with a thick fat chin always stay at home and take care of the kids while those moms with a pointy chin always stay out and leave the responsibility of raising the kids to the maids.

Fu Er and Gui Lai ⏤ Fu Er and Gui Lai are the reading points for filial relationship.

Fullness at both Fu Er and Gui Lai means such mother is popular among the children. She can enjoy a peaceful and enjoyable life in the final years with all the kids by her side. Her luck is even better if she also has a round fleshy chin.

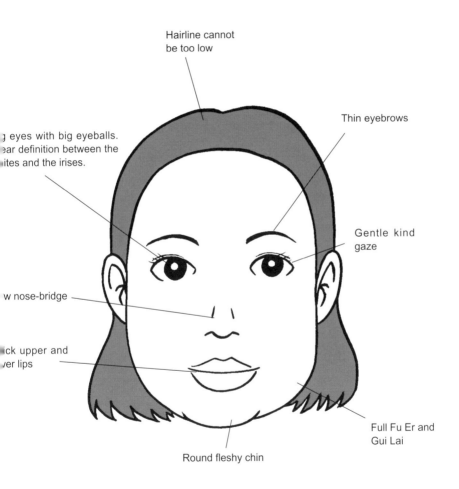

Hairline cannot
be too low

Thin eyebrows

g eyes with big eyeballs.
ear definition between the
ites and the irises.

Gentle kind
gaze

w nose-bridge

ick upper and
ver lips

Full Fu Er and
Gui Lai

Round fleshy chin

21. Features of a good father

A good father actually shares many common features with a good mother and such features are listed as follows:

Forehead — A high hairline with particularly high points at the corners of the forehead. It means the person has strong analytical power and can analyze the problems for the children in great details. He would then let the children decide for themselves with appropriate guidance.

Low hairline with narrow forehead means the person is stubborn and always insists in his own views. Such father always makes his children follow his footsteps so that the children become inflexible and unable to cope with changes.

Eyebrows — He should have neat eyebrows with brow hair growing close to the brow bones. As such eyebrows mean he is thoughtful and patient and he will not lose temper easily.

On the contrary, messy brow hair means the person is confused in thinking and cannot organize things in an orderly manner. He is also illogical and unreasonable. In case he also has protruding brow bones, he has bad temper and impulsive character, which makes him more likely to beat the children.

Eyes — Big eyeballs mean the person is kind at heart. A high-spirit look in the eyes means he is decisive. A gentle gaze means the person is virtuous, kind and patience. Either one of the above makes a good father. Of course a father with all three traits is the best. Small eyeballs like "3-white" or "4-white" eyes mean the person is bad tempered and impatient. Eyes with a ferocious look mean the person is cold and unattached. He is likely to abandon his kids.

Nose — Men usually have taller nose-bridge than women. Tall nose-bridge means strong self esteem and that should not be a problem for a man. A bumpy nose-bridge or a nose-bridge too low, on the other hand, is not a good nose for a father. Bumps on the nose-bridge means he is short-tempered and impulsive while a low nose bridge means he lacks self confidence and he withdraws whenever some problems arise. Both of them do not make a good father.

Mouth — Men usually have thinner upper lips and thicker lower lips, which means they care more about gratification of desire. It is okay as long as they have a balanced mouth shape implying they are careful in language. Neatly grown front teeth further enhance his potential as a good father because they are signs of credibility and honesty. On the contrary, those with crooked mouth and sparsely grown teeth talk nonsense all the time and always break their promises to the children.

Chin — A round fleshy chin slightly bulging forward means the person likes to stay at home and communicate with the children. He has good relationship and compatibility with his children who treat him as a friend. On the other hand, a pointy receding chin means a lack of communication with his children. He has a remote cold relationship with his children because he does not like to stay at home.

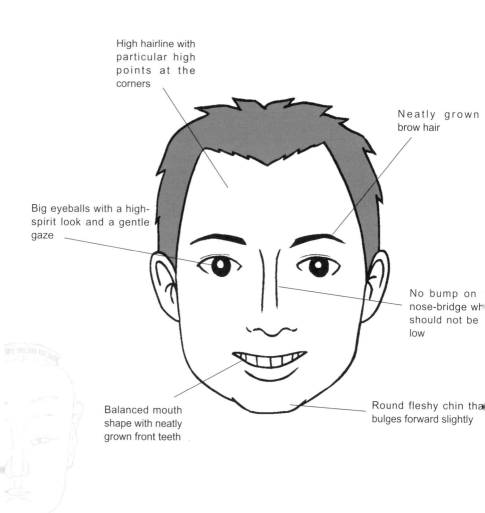

High hairline with particular high points at the corners

Neatly grown brow hair

Big eyeballs with a high-spirit look and a gentle gaze

No bump on nose-bridge wh should not be low

Balanced mouth shape with neatly grown front teeth

Round fleshy chin tha bulges forward slightly

22. Features of incompatibility with parents

There are many signs that a person is not compatible with his/her parents. By "incompatible", we mean the person is separated from his/her parents since an early age, or the person has a very poor relationship with his/her parents.

▪ *Incompatibility with the father*

1. 3 horizontal lines on the forehead:

2. A mole at Tian Zhong:

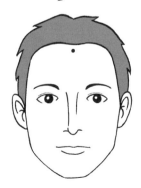

3. A mole at Xin Tang:

4. A mole at Si Kong:

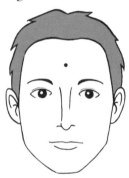

5. Spiral hair on the hairline:

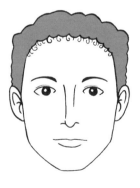

6. Extremely low hairline:

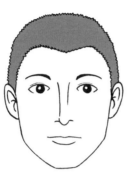

7. Horseshoe hairline:

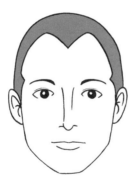

8. A downward notch on the hairline:

9. A depression or a scar at the Sun Corner:

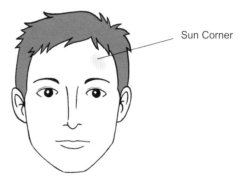

Sun Corner

10. Thick eyebrows growing too close to the eyes:

11. Spiral hair on the left eyebrow:

12. A vertical line running from the forehead to Xin Tang:

13. A nose obviously crooked to the left:

14. A left cheekbone that protrudes, or is crooked, low or depressed:

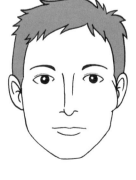

15. A left ear grown in a low position, is extremely small, flipping backwards, or the upper rim is pointing upward:

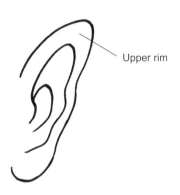

Upper rim

16. A missing left front teeth since an early age:

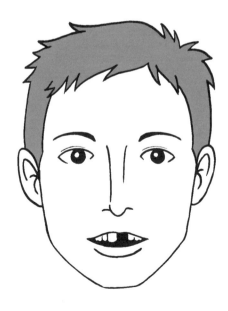

Incompatibility with the mother

1. A mole at Tian Ting:

2. A depression, or a scar at the Moon Corner:

Moon corner

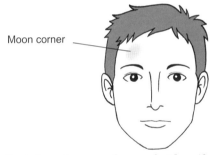

3. A low depressed nose-bridge (for males only):

4. A nose obviously crooked to the right:

5. A right cheekbone that protrudes, or is crooked, low or depressed:

In the ancient time, if a person was considered incompatible to his/her parents, he/she would ask someone to be his/her godfather or godmother, or even would demand the God to be his/her godfather, so as to spread out the incompatibility and minimize the incompatibility to his/her biological mother/father.

Remember such incompatibility does not mean the child's birth will cause bad luck to the parents. It only refers to their offspring-parents relationship and the health of the parents.

23. Choosing the right employee

■ *Maid*

Before picking an employee, make sure you know what purpose his/her job serves. Say, when you hire a domestic helper, no matter she is a Filipino, Thai or Indonesian maid, the first criterion is big eyes with big eyeballs. She would be righteous and honest without shady intentions. She would also be gentle and sentimental. A domestic helper with big eyeballs will never abuse your kids.

On the other hand, small eyes with small eyeballs mean the person hides her feelings from others. Even if she is unhappy about something, she would not say a word. She is also ruthless and revengeful, which means she would channel her anger or discontent onto your kids.

Her nose-bridge should be low as tall nose-bridge means the person has high self esteem and is difficult to get along with. Low nose-bridge means she is willing to accept comments and she is optimistic and hard working. She would not complain even if she works extremely hard.

Her face should be round in shape as those with round faces love to stay at home. She also has good human relationship. On the other hand, a maid with a pointy face cannot tolerate staying at home all day and will not adapt to the life of a domestic helper.

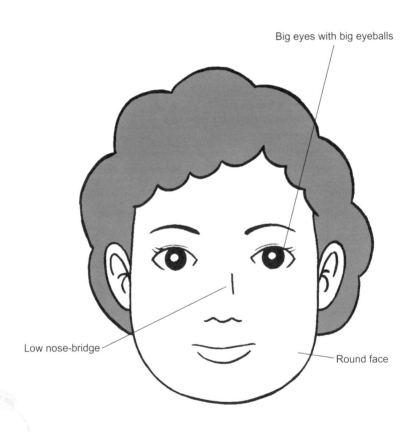

■ *Driver*

Hiring a driver is somewhat the same as hiring a maid. Pick one with big eyes and big eyeballs, low nose-bridge and round face. If the driver has to double as a bodyguard, the requirements will be different.

■ *Bodyguard*

The first criterion will be a tall straight nose-bridge as it means the person has a strong sense of justice and responsibility. Such bodyguard will not abandon his boss in crisis. Wide jawbones mean he can keep secrets and will not disclose his boss' location. Moreover, those with wide jawbones are usually healthy and swift in actions.

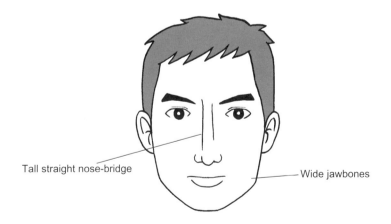

Tall straight nose-bridge

Wide jawbones

■ *Housekeeper*

A housekeeper is different from a maid as he/she has to take care of all the routine matters in the house and lead a group of maids. Therefore, he/she should have a slightly tall straight nose-bridge, "strong" looking eyes, big eyeballs, tightly closed lips and an air of sternness, so that he can control and manage the maids.

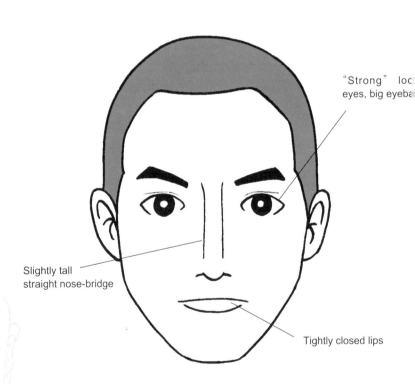

"Strong" loc
eyes, big eyeba

Slightly tall
straight nose-bridge

Tightly closed lips

24. Read the white of the eyes

The eyes are the windows to the soul and you can take a peep at a person's psyche through his/her eyes. Yet, it takes much professional judgment in reading the "look" of the eyes. On the other hand, reading quantifiable aspects such as the size of the eyeballs and the position of an eyeball in the eye are a lot easier.

Most people have their eyeballs covered by the eyelids at the top and bottom and the white is on both the left and right sides of the eyeballs. Such eyes are normal. Those eyeballs surrounded by the white on more than two sides are not common.

1. "2-white" but slightly skewed — "2-white" means the eyeballs are surrounded by the white on left and right, which is normal. Yet, such person has one eyeball off the centre of the eye when he/she look straight ahead. This cannot be easily noticed unless you stand right in front of the person and ask him/her to look straight at you.

Such reading means the person's ancestor was extremely wealthy but had killed somebody. The ancestor could not have a good life in his final years and rubbed bad Feng Shui on the offspring. Therefore, the offspring is likely to live far apart from and lose contact with each other.

People having such eyes should do more charitable and virtuous things to rectify the bad influence from the ancestor.

2. Crossed eyes — It means both eyeballs are skewed toward the inner corners of the eye.

Such person usually has poor health and might be abandoned by his/her parents since early childhood. He/she also has poor health in the elderly years.

People having such eyes should do more exercise and strengthen the bodies to get rid of such destiny.

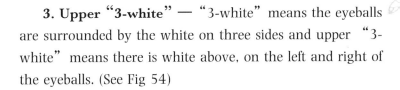

3. Upper "3-white" — "3-white" means the eyeballs are surrounded by the white on three sides and upper "3-white" means there is white above, on the left and right of the eyeballs. (See Fig 54)

Such eyes are not common and classical documents on face-reading has it that "upper 3-white means cunningness; lower 3-white means criminal affairs".

Thus, those with upper "3-white" eyes are usually evil at heart and would go in the wrong way. Even though they might be born to a rich family and might have excellent education, they still could not escape the inherent negative quality in their psyche. Use care if you meet someone with such eyes.

Fig 54: Upper "3-white"   **Fig 55: Lower "3-white"**

4. Lower "3-white" — It means there is white below, on the left and the right of the eyeballs. (See Fig 55)

Such person has a strong desire to win and will do anything to get what he/she wants. Thus, he/she actually has a good chance to be successful. Yet, his/her persistence and determination to achieve his/her goal without caring about others makes more enemies than friends. That is why classical documents on face reading says, "lower 3-white is likely to die from violence," because of his/her personality. If he/she can learn when to retreat without going too far, such person might escape from some dangers.

Such eyes are also signs of "disastrous love," which means the person easily give up everything in pursuit of the opposite sex. That's why a Chinese old saying goes like, "even the fittest warrior cannot resist the temptation of beauty."

5. "4-white" — It means the eyeballs are extremely small when compared with the whole eyes. There is the white on all four sides of the eyeballs.

25. Different shapes of the eyes

Other than the white of the eyes, read also the size and length for a person's characters.

1. Big eyes with big eyeballs — Big eyes mean the person is strong in expressing his/her feelings; while big eyeballs mean he/she is innocent and gentle in nature like children. Such person likes to ask questions all the time and that is why people call such eyes "child's eyes."

2. Small eyes with small eyeballs — Small eyes mean the person keeps his/her feelings to him/herself and does not show his/her true self easily.

Small eyeballs mean the person is self-centred, selfish, revengeful and he/she remembers who treats him/her bad forever.

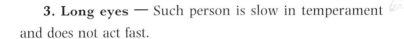

3. Long eyes — Such person is slow in temperament and does not act fast.

He/she is gentle and easy going.

He/she is likely to have many potential love affairs.

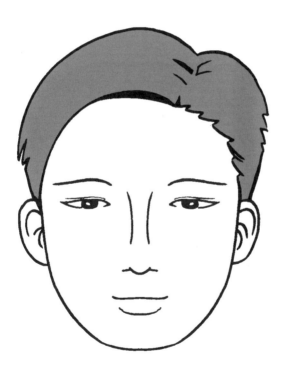

4. Short eyes ─ Such person is short-tempered and acts fast.

He/she has to put things to an end in the quickest possible ways and do not hide his/her feelings.

He/she shows every sentiment on his/her face.

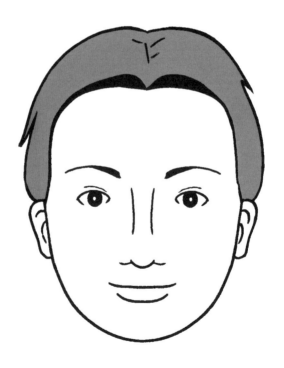

5. Triangular eyes — It can be further classified into upper triangular eyes (i.e.the upper eyelid forms an angle on top of the eye) and lower triangular eyes (i.e. the lower eyelid forms an angle at the bottom of the eye).

Upper triangular eyes means the person will lose money due to fraudulent behaviour around the age of 35 or 36. The lower triangular eyes usually happen to the elderly as their muscle collapses to form an angle below the eye.

People having such eyes are especially gullible and are prone to frauds. If your family members have such eyes, make sure you remind them to be alert about any financial loss due to fraudulent crimes.

Upper triangular eyes

  muscles sagging

Lower triangular eyes

26. Acnes mean something

Everybody has acnes once in a while — sometimes they appear on the body and sometimes they appear on the face. Actually acnes on different locations of the body have different implications on luck.

■ Forehead

Acnes on the forehead mostly tell predestined issues.

For instance, acnes in the Bian Cheng area on the left and Yi Ma area on the right mean the person will face some problems and frustration in his/her trip.

Acnes at Qiu Ling or Zhong Mu means the person will face some problems if he/she goes on a worshipping trip for his/her ancestor or for god.

Acnes on the left forehead mean the person's father is having a bad mood or is sick.

Acnes on the right forehead mean the person's mother is having a bad mood or is sick.

Acnes right above the outer brow ends mean the person will be in financial difficulty soon.

Acnes right above the inner brow ends mean the person is having financial problems at that moment.

Acnes on the temples mean the person has to use his/her saving some for reason.

Acnes on Xin Tang mean the person is having a bad mood and is engaged in fights frequently.

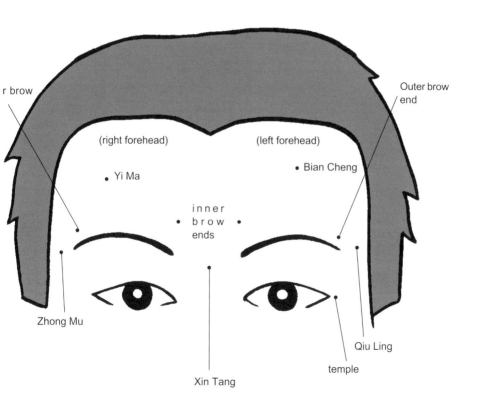

■ *Eyebrows and the eyes*

Acnes on the eyebrows near the inner brow ends mean the person is having a bad mood and is always engaged in fights.

Acnes on the eyebrows near the outer brow ends mean the person is likely to lose money because of his/her friends. He/she also is having a bad time in relationship.

Acnes near the inner eye corners mean the person is having arguments with his/her spouse. He/she is also engaged in other arguments associated with the opposite sex.

Acnes near the outer eye corner on the left mean frequent arguments with others for guys, while acnes near the outer eye corner on the right mean the same for women.

Acnes in between the eyes and the eyebrows imply poor atmosphere at home due to mishaps.

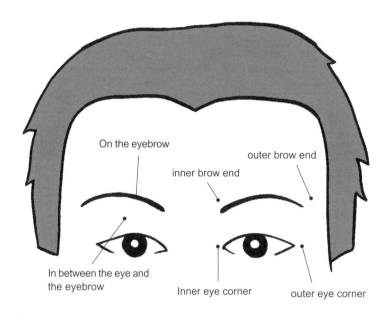

■ *The nose and cheekbones*

Acnes at Shan Gen on the nose-bridge mean arguments between husband and wife.

Acnes at Nian Shang mean the person will be sick shortly.

Acnes at Shou Shang mean someone from the person's family is sick.

Acnes on the left side of the nose mean the person has problems on his/her relationship that are caused by the male side. Those on the right side mean the same problems caused by the female side.

Acnes on the nose tip mean the person will have to spend extra money on regular expenditure items, such as clothing or interior decoration.

Acnes on the nose wings mean the person will have to spend extra money on irregular events, such as traffic penalty tickets or other expenditure out of bad luck.

Acnes on the cheekbones mean the person has bad credit at the time and has poor human relationship.

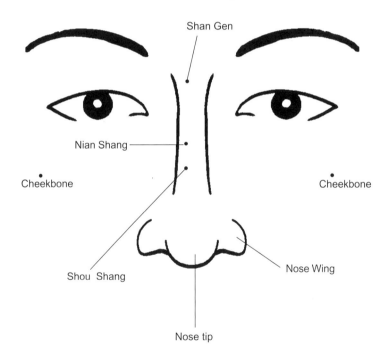

Shan Gen

Nian Shang

Cheekbone

Cheekbone

Shou Shang

Nose Wing

Nose tip

■ *Mouth*

Acnes on the upper lip mean someone is taking advantage of this person by asking him/her to pay for meals. In case there are many acnes on the upper lip, the person might have unsatisfactory sex life.

Acnes around the mouth corners mean the person is having argument with someone. Acnes below the mouth corners mean the person spends too much lately. Acnes right below the centre of the lower lip mean the person is prone to digestive problems.

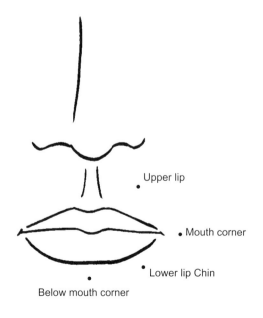

Upper lip

Mouth corner

Lower lip Chin

Below mouth corner

Chin

Acnes on the chin mean there is some moving in the person's house, such as moving the furniture around.

Acnes in the left and right area of subordinates mean the person's subordinates are disobedient and do not take orders smoothly.

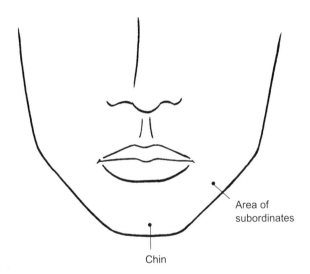

Area of subordinates

Chin

Ear

Acnes on any part of the ear mean the person is annoyed.

169

27. Read the hair

The hair plays an important part in face reading as it tells a person's character, relationship with parents, spousal relationship, health and general luck.

■ *Character*

Fine and soft hair means the person is gentle in nature. He/she is willing to accept others' comments and forgive others' shortcomings. He/she does not remember how others treat him/her bad and he/she is likely to be the one who gives up in times of argument.

Thick dry and tough hair means the person is stubborn and always insists on his/her own view. Such person is inflexible, impulsive and impatient. Yet, he/she has stamina and is hard working.

High hairline, especially the hairline retreating at the corners of the forehead, means the person is highly analytical, flexible, intelligent and intellectual.

The lower the hairline, the more stubborn a person is. He/she is also inflexible, unwilling to listen to comments and has poor analytical power. Such person is likely to have arguments with others all his/her life and is difficult to get along with. This also applies to those with hard curly hair.

■ *Relationship with parents*

Those having a neat hairline not too low usually have good relationship with parents. Those with a low hairline (See Fig 56), indented hairline (Fig 57), horseshoe hairline (Fig 58), a downward notch in the hairline (Fig 59), premature grey hair or thick dense tough hair, usually have only remote relationship with the father.

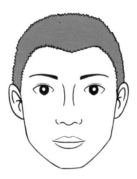

Fig 56: Low hairline

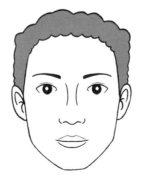

Fig 57: Indented hairline

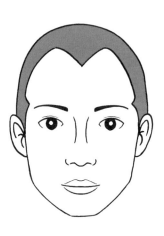

Fig 58: Horseshoe hairline

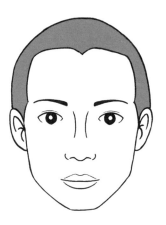

Fig 59: A downward notch on the hairline

■ *Health*

Shiny hair means the person is healthy. Dry yellow hair implies poor circulation and bad health condition. Sudden hair loss means the person will have a major sickness soon. Originally shiny hair suddenly turning dry and yellow, or black hair sudden turning grey also foretells a person's major sickness.

■ *Spousal relationship*

Fine and soft hair means the person has good spousal relationship. Thick and dry hair means the person has poor spousal relationship. If one of the couple has fine hair while the other has tough hair, the one with fine hair always yields to the other in times of argument.

Women with dry yellow hair are incompatible with their husbands. They have remote spousal relationship and cannot benefit from the husbands' success. Women whose hair smells no matter how often they wash it are destined to be broke and they also adversely influence the husbands' luck.

Women with thick dense hair do not have good influence on luck from the husbands and have poor spousal relationship.

Men with thick dense hair do not understand the implications of love affairs.

■ *General Luck*

Fine, soft and shiny hair means the person can get help from important people all his/her life. They have smooth luck without many frustrations or accidents.

Thick tough hair means the person has to work hard for money and he/she has to work twice as hard to have the same achievements as others.

Low hairline means the person is not good at study and he/she has poor luck in youth ages. He/she is unlikely to have achievements before the age of 30. This also applies to those with indented hairline.

Hair loss that starts at the forehead is a sign of the person's luck turning good.

Hair loss that starts on top of the head is a sign of the person's luck turning bad.

Sudden hair loss in one patch or several patches like the size of a 50-cent coin, means the person is extremely worried.

28. Read the nose

What kind of women is especially prone to divorce and poor spousal relationship? What kind of men can make most money out of nothing? You don't need their birth dates and time. You only need to look at their noses.

■ *Roman nose: women likely to divorce*

Features: It is a long nose with a bump on the nose-bridge. It is so named as many Romans had such noses.

Women with Roman nose usually have poor luck of marriage. As the nose is the location of marriage for women (while it is the location of luck of wealth for men), a bumpy nose-bridge means such women will not yield to the husbands in times of argument. That is why they are likely to get divorced. Guys with such nose are diligent and will try their best to solve problems. Men with such nose are likely to have successful career.

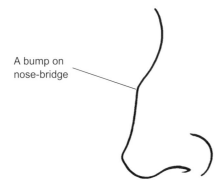

A bump on nose-bridge

■ *Jewish nose: making lots of money with little investment*

Features: It means the nose-bridge arches slightly upward while the nose tip is round, fleshy and overhanging. It is so named because it is common among Jewish people.

Men with such nose are mostly cunning and calculating. They will develop big business out of the smallest budget. Yet, they are usually misers.

Women with such nose usually lead a happy life and they also make money if they start their own business.

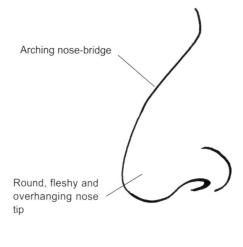

Arching nose-bridge

Round, fleshy and overhanging nose tip

■ *Nose of second wives: women enjoy much of the husbands' love and wealth*

Features: It is a short nose with flat nose-bridge and a round fleshy nose tip.

Being a first wife, a woman with such nose either works very hard for the husband her whole life or she would get divorced. Yet, being a second wife (i.e. married to a divorced or widowed man), she would enjoy all her husband's wealth and love and have excellent marriage.

Men with such nose work hard but without much pay-off. They are unlikely to be successful.

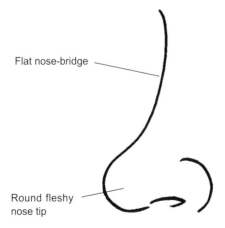

Flat nose-bridge

Round fleshy nose tip

■ *Eagle-beak nose: keen on helping friends*

Features: It is a nose with arching nose-bridge and a pointy small nose tip pointing downward. It looks like the beak of an eagle.

Men with such nose are active and diligent. They would pay anything to achieve their goals. When their friends seek help from them, they always try their best to help. Such person has the best development in less popular businesses or those jobs involving major ups and downs.

Women with such nose are mostly short-tempered and violent. They are unlikely to have good marriage.

Arching nose-bridge

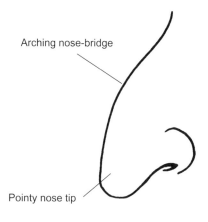

Pointy nose tip

■ *Wine goblet nose: a strong sense of justice and being scared of his wife*

Features: Shan Gen (in between the nose bridge and the eyes) is narrow while the nose tip is wide and big without obvious nose wings.

A man with such nose has a strong sense of justice and responsibility, but he is scared of his wife. He also has stamina to carry on in adverse conditions. He can accumulate some wealth.

A woman with such nose can help her husband's career but she has high self esteem which makes her difficult to get along with. She might not have very good marriage relationship.

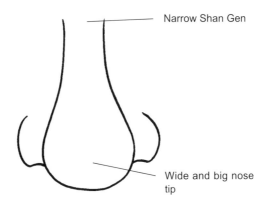

Narrow Shan Gen

Wide and big nose tip

■ *Child nose: innocent and naîve*

Features: The nose bridge is low while the nose tip points upward.

Such person has the character of a child. She loves raising questions on everything and she falls in love with older men.

Guys with such nose are too naîve and too impractical to encounter the real world. They are unlikely to be successful.

Women with such nose should marry older guys to have a happy marriage.

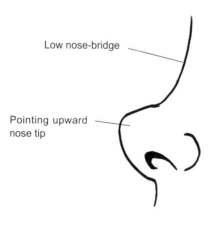

Low nose-bridge

Pointing upward
nose tip

29. Read the lips

Common lips in men

▪ *Rectangular lips*

Features: Upper and lower lips of equal thickness form a slightly rectangular shape (with 4 obvious corners).

Personality: The person is careful in language and has potential to work in the government. He has a strong sense of responsibility and would not abandon his family.

In case he also has neatly grown teeth without gap in between, he is truly the man you can rely on.

■ *God of Thunder's lips*

Features: It means long philtrum (the groove between the nose and the lips) and slightly pointy lips.

Personality: The person is stubborn, persistent and slightly sexist, but he also has a strong sense of justice.

Such man has poor relationship with his children and wife. He also adversely affects his wife's luck.

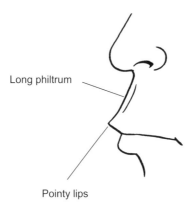

Long philtrum

Pointy lips

Common lips in women

■ *Cat fight lips*

Features: It means the person has thin lips and the centre of her upper lip forms a pointy projection.

Personality: She likes to argue with people on all possible issues and she never yields even when she does not have a point. That is why she is always involved in troubles.

Pointy projection

■ *Singing lips*

Features: It means thick lips with many lines.

Personality: Although she has a talent for singer, she is never a good speaker.

She should not talk too much to avoid the chance of offending others.

She is also prone to digestive system problems.

Thick lips with lines

Common lips in both men and women

■ *New moon lips*

Features: The mouth corners point upward when the mouth is closed.

Personality: The person is optimistic with mild temper. He/she makes a perfect husband/wife.

Such person also has excellent luck in the elderly years.

Pointy upward
mouth corners

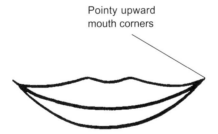

185

Inverted boat lips

Features: The mouth corners point downward when the mouth is closed.

Personality: Coupling with a big fat chin, such mouth means wealth and fame. Yet, the person will adversely affect the spouse's luck and have poor relationship with the children.

Without a big fat chin, such person would be pessimistic and have poor spousal relationship. He/she will lead a lonely broke life in the final years.

Pointy downward
mouth corners

186

▪ *Curling lips*

Features: Such lips obviously curl upward.

Personality: The person is strong in language and he/ she knows how to flatter.

Such person should work in jobs that require talking skills.

Curling upward lips

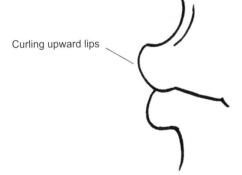

■ *Crooked lips*

Features: The mouth is obviously skewed to one side (except those caused by diseases or accidents).

Personality: Such person lies all the time and he/she always breaks his/her promises. In case the person also has gaps between the front teeth, never believe a word he/she says.

Skewed mouth

■ *"Woman with big mouths eats until the husband is broke"?*

This proverb is no longer valid from modern face reading point of view. Big mouth means the person is an extrovert with strong socializing skills and daring character. Small mouth means the person is an introvert with conservative and cowardly character. In the ancient time, women with big mouth were not accepted because women should only stay at home and take care of the house chores. Yet, nowadays, working women with big mouths actually have a better career than those with small mouths.

30. Natural born liars

Some people love to lie and lying is part of their lives. They even lie so much that they start to believe in what they say and don't notice that they are lying.

There are two kinds of liars — one with intrinsic predisposition; the other is simply too talkative and meaning gets lost in the way. The following is a checklist of facial features that imply strong potential of being a liar.

■ *Basic features of liars*

1. Big gaps between front teeth — Such person are talkative and as he/she talks too much and there is a higher chance that he/she misinterprets or misleads people by accident. He/she is also a bragger without noticing his/her lying habits.

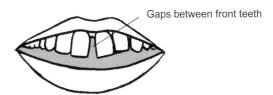

Gaps between front teeth

2. Crooked mouth ⏤ No matter the person has crooked mouth when he/she is talking or not, he/she is a natural born liar anyway.

Such person does not even know he/she him/herself is lying and they are so confused about truth and lies that they cannot tell the difference.

Those who have crooked mouth because of external causes like disease or accidents are exceptions.

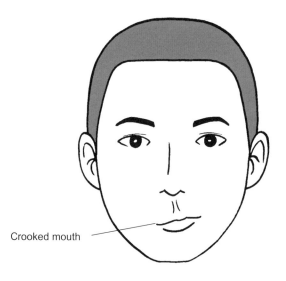

Crooked mouth

3. Slightly protruding eyes with a round face — Such person is born to be talkative. He/she talks no matter the things are meaningful or nonsense. He/she would pretend he/she understands even though if that is not the case and always pretends to be the expert on everything. That's why such person is always annoying.

Those who have protruding eyes because of shortsightedness or prolonged wearing of spectacles are exceptions.

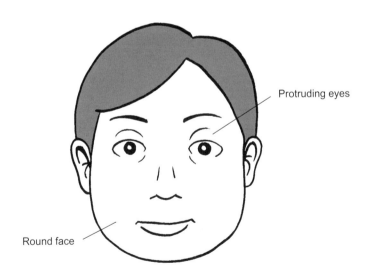

Protruding eyes

Round face

4. Upper lip globe — An obvious globe shape at the centre of the upper lip means the person loves to talk and will never yield in arguments even though he/she does not have a point. He/she will go on and on until the opponent gives up. In case the person also has bad front teeth, he/she is likely to become a liar.

Obvious globe shape

5. Small and pointy tongue — The person is born to be talkative and loves to gossip.

In case he/she also has gaps between the front teeth, he/she would tend to have serious lying problems.

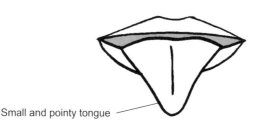

Small and pointy tongue

6. Blow torch lips — This typical depiction of nosy woman in comic books has both lips protruding forward as if the person is blowing a candle. People with such mouth are talkative and nosy. They are strong at arguing and you'd better not talk to such people.

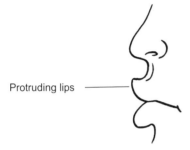

Protruding lips

7. Protruding front teeth with gum exposed — Teeth sticking out mean the person is talkative and exposed gum means the person cannot keep secrets. The two traits work together to make this person talk nonsense all the time, brag about everything and turn truth into lies.

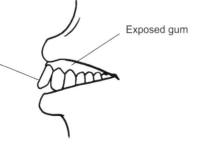

Exposed gum

Protuding front teeth

8. Thin upper lip or upper lip curling upward ― The person has born talking skills.

In case he or she also has unsteady gaze or crooked mouth, he or she is likely to be a habitual liar.

As such person has strong language skills, it would not be easy to discover his or her lies.

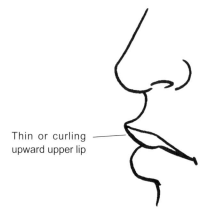

Thin or curling ――――
upward upper lip

Habitual Liars Top 5

- Crooked mouth

- Gaps between front teeth

- Round face with protruding eyes

- Blow torch mouth

- Protruding front teeth

Talkative People Top 5

(those who have these features plus the features of habitual liars will become extremely skillful liars)

- Upper lip globe

- Small pointy tongue

- Upper lip that curls up

- Thin upper lip

- Gum exposed

■ *How to tell a person is lying?*

1. Blinking and smiling — If a person keeps blinking his/her eyes when talking to you, it means he/she is very nervous. He/she also smiles to cover up his/her stress.

The two actions reveal the person is lying.

2. Looking around — A person who looks around when talking to you does not really want to communicate with you. Otherwise, he/she does not mean what he/she says. He/she is just trying to figure out how to give the right response, but not his/her true response.

3. Lowering his/her head before talking — Lowering head means the person is thinking. Thinking before talking means he/she rephrases his/her thought before saying it.

Such person does not say what he/she really means. Do not trust his/her words.

31. The mystery of moles

Many people have moles on their faces. Did you know these pigment spots affect the luck of your whole life? An idiom says, "there is no friendly mole on the face." Any mole on the face means something negative.

■ *The Ear*

It is divided into the rim, the inner ridge, the earlobe, the flap cover and the area in front of the ear.

The rim — A mole on the rim means the person is smart and has active thinking.

The inner ridge — A mole here means longevity and enhancement of health condition.

The back of the ear — A mole here means filial virtues and the person has better relationship with parents.

The earlobe — A mole here means the person has good luck of wealth, can accumulate wealth and will have excellent luck after the age of 60.

In front of the ear — A mole in front of the left ear means poor health before the age of 30 while a mole in front of the right ear opening means poor health after the age of 30.

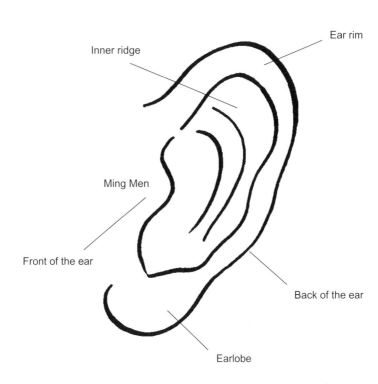

Inner ridge

Ear rim

Ming Men

Front of the ear

Back of the ear

Earlobe

The Forehead

There are 13 reading points in the forehead representing different things:

Huo Xing and Tian Zhong — A mole at either position means the person is poor at study around the age of 15 or 16.

He/she has to quit school and work early and has poor relationship with the father. He or she should study abroad or work part-time or work during the summer vacation.

Sun and Moon Corners — A mole at either position means the person's parents do not have good health or good relationship. The Sun Corner refers to the father while the Moon Corner refers to the mother.

Tian Ting — A mole here means other people will not positively enhance this person's luck. He or she also has poor relationship with the father and has to work hard by himself for success.

Fu Jiao and Bian Cheng — These are the reading points for traveling luck.

A mole at either position means the person does not have good development in foreign countries and unhappy events would happen to him/her even if he/she travels on vacation.

Si Kong and Zhong Zheng — These are the locations of government career. Those with a mole at either position do not have good development in the government and should find jobs that are outdoors in nature or they should work hard on their own for success.

Such person also has poor relationship with his or her parents.

Qiu Ling and Zhong Mu — These points represent the influence from the psychic world. A mole at either position means the person's ancestor is not buried at a location with good Feng Shui.

The person also faces difficulties if he or she wants to go on a trip to worship the god.

Xin Tang — It is the area of hope and a mole here means the person is pessimistic and cannot adapt to the fast changes of the society. He or she also has remote relationship with parents, but he or she would have substantial achievements.

The temples — A mole at either temple means the person loves to retreat into the wildness. It also means the person cannot accumulate wealth before the age of 30.

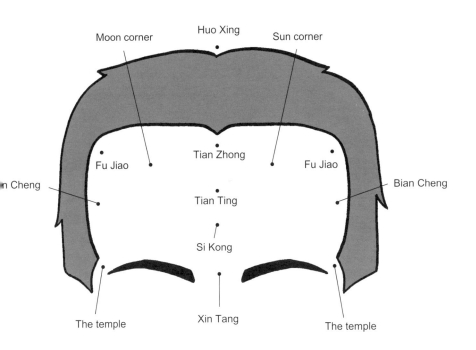

■ *The eyes and the eyebrows*

This area covers the brow bones, eyebrows, Jiao Suo, E Lu, Fu Tang, Long Gong, the eyes themselves and Wo Can.

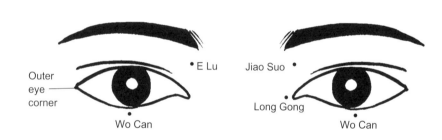

Left and right brow bones — These reading points are actually independent from the eyebrows unless your brow hair grows right on the brow bones, then the brow bones and the eyebrows are referring to the same locations.

Good brow bones should be bright and any mole on them means the brightness is hindered and the person cannot develop him/herself to the full potential. Yet, a flat mole is covered by brow hair becomes a neutral sign and the person is intelligent.

If the mole is raised, it is a bad sign that the person has to be separated from his siblings or his siblings die early. His/her hands get wounded easily — a raised mole on the left brow bone means the left hand gets hurt easily while one on the right means the same thing for the right hand.

Left and right eyebrows — There is a fallacy in the public that they call a mole covered in brow hair "a pearl covered in straw" — meaning such person is precious and not showy. Yet, this is only a rumour just like moles under the feet mean power, and moles on the chest mean grand aspirations, which is not true at all.

In fact, moles in the brow hair mean the person has the potential to be intelligent, but it is not the determinant factor to read a person's intelligence. You have to read whether his/her brow hair is fine and neatly grown; and whether there is a "strong" high-spirited look in his/her eyes before you can really tell if he/she is intelligent. Moles covered by dense brow hair mean the person is prone to accidents associated with water while those covered in thin sparsely grown brow hair mean the person is prone to accidents associated with fire.

Read the ages in which such accidents are more likely to occur by whether the mole is on the left or right: age 1, 10, 19, 28, 37, 46 and 55 if it is on the left brow; age 7, 16, 25, 34, 43, 52 and 61 if it is on the right.

Jiao Suo and E Lu — These are the positions right below the inner brow ends. Moles at these points mean the person is likely to suffer from imprisonment at a certain point of his/her life (or detention for more 24 hours). Read the ages in which such imprisonment is more likely to happen the same way as the eyebrows.

Area of familial relationship — This is located between the eyes and the eyebrows and it tells the relationship among family members. The wider the area (i.e. the eye and eyebrow are further apart), the more important family relationships are to the person.

People having the eyes grown close to the eyebrows usually have remote family relationship (including siblings and parents.) No matter the area is wide or not, any mole in the area means the person cannot inherit the estates from the family.

Fu Tang — These are the area right above the eyebrows. A mole at the inner Fu Tang (near the inner brow end) means the person has to encounter sudden short of funds often. A mole at the outer Fu Tang (near the outer brow end) means the person has to face long term financial problems such as gathering fund for investment or buying real estate.

Long Gong — These are points near the inner eye corners and moles at such points mean the person has problems in love relationships always, especially at the age of 32, 35 and 36.

Outer eye corners — These are the areas of spousal relationship and they also tell the health conditions of the wife and husband. A mole around the left outer eye corner means poor spousal relationship or the husband has poor health (likely to happen at age 23, 32, 41 and 50), while one on the right means the same for the wife (likely to happen at age 17, 26, 35, 44 and 53).

Please note the outer eye corners govern luck at age 39 and 40 and people with moles at these spots have even more serious problems in relationship in those years.

Triple Yang and Triple Yin — These are the areas inside the eye: the left eye is Yang while the right eye is Yin.

Any mole or spot in the white of the eyes means the person gets involved in arguments and incidents associated with the opposite sex, such as adultery and multiple relationships.

A mole on the white of left eye means such incidents happen before the age of 30 while one on the white of the right eye means they happen after age 30.

Wo Can — These are the bags under the eyes. A mole on the bag under the left eye means the person has poor relationship with his/her sons while one on the right means the poor relationship with his/her daughters.

If the mole is under the left inner eye corner, it means bad relationship with the oldest son. A mole under the centre of the left eye means poor relationship with the second son while the one under the left outer eye corner means the third son. The same applies to the right eye for daughters.

■ *Nose and cheekbones*

This area includes Shan Gen, Jing She, Guang Dian, Nian Shang, Shou Shang, husband and wife points, nose tip, left and right nose wings, left and right cheekbones.

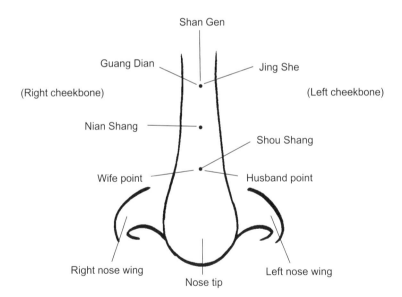

Shan Gen — A mole at Shan Gen is a crucial sign of bad marriage and a raised mole is especially so.

Such mole means stressful love relationships all his/her life and the possibility of divorce. Relationship crises are particularly likely to happen at age 20, 29, 38, 41 and 44. Those with a mole at Shan Gen usually have to wait till age 45 afterward for stable relationships.

Jing She and Guang Dian — These are the points on the left and right of Shan Gen respectively.

A mole at either point means the person has problems with his/her urinary system, including kidney and bladder diseases. Such person also encounters barriers in love relationships and might involve in sexual scandals.

Nian Shang and Shou Shang — They are called the area of sickness and mishaps.

A mole at Nian Shang means his/her family members get sick easily while a mole at Shou Shang means the person him/herself is sick all the time and should do more exercise to strengthen the body.

Husband point and wife point — Husband point is on the left side of the nose while wife point is on the right side.

A mole at the husband point means the person has relationship problems all his/her life and the problems are mostly caused by the husband. Similarly, a mole at the wife point means the same and the problems are mostly caused by the wife. Read the paragraph on Shan Gen for the ages in which problems are likely to happen.

Nose tip — This is the reading point for the luck of stable wealth.

A mole on the nose tip means the person has to spend lots of money on regular expenses. He/she is also likely to give birth to a son with a successful future.

Left and right nose wings — They are the reading points for the luck of unstable income.

A mole on the left nose wing means the person suffers from accidental loss of money before the age of 30. A mole on the right means the same after the age of 30.

Left and right cheekbones — These are the areas that tell a person's authority and human relationship.

A mole on either area means the person always gets troubles from friends and subordinates. Those troubles are especially serious and likely to happen at age 46 and 47. Take special care in those years.

■ *The mouth*

This area includes Shi Cang, Lu Cang, philtrum, the lips, mouth corners and Cheng Jiang.

Shi Cang and Lu Cang — They are located above the upper lip below the nose.

A mole in the area means the person loves to treat others to meals and he/she is likely spend lots of money for that purpose all his/her life.

Philtrum — It is the depressed groove between the upper lip and the nose at the centre.

It tells the relationship with the offspring and a mole at this position means the person has remote relationship with the sons and daughters. The relationship is especially poor after age 51.

The lips — A mole on the lips is called "eating" mole and it means the person has luck for good food.

Yet, a mole on the lip line of the upper lip means the person has problems with digestive systems such as intestinal tumours. He/she should pay more attention to any relevant symptoms.

Mouth corners — A mole at the mouth corner is a "gossip" mole. Such person is nosy and loves gossiping, which

could get him/her into trouble.

A mole below the mouth corner means the person always has a shortage of fund, but it does not mean the person is broke. Even though if he/she is rich, he/she still feels he/she does not have enough money.

Cheng Jiang — This is the area right below the lower lip. A mole at this spot means the person has problems with his/her digestive system.

In case he/she cannot drink but loves to drink, he/she is likely to suffer from food poisoning and diarrhea.

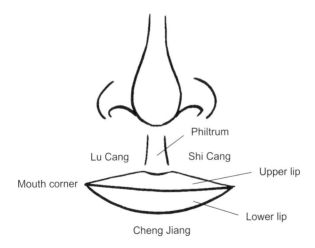

■ *The chin*

This area covers Di Ge, area of subordinates, left and right dimples, and left and right Gui Lai.

Di Ge — It means the whole chin and it also refers to the family. A mole in the area looks like a hole in the house and literally the person's home (or homes of his/her family members) must have leaking problems, say, in the window sills, or in the water tank of the washroom.

Area of subordinates — (also known as left and right Di Ku) These are the reading points to see if the person's servants and subordinates are capable and obedient.

A mole in either point means the servants and subordinates are incapable or disobedient. A mole on the left Di Ku refers to incapability of male servant while one on the right means a female servant is unhelpful.

Gui Lai — This is the area to read if the person's sons and daughters would be by his/her side in his/her elderly years. A mole at this spot means the person has remote relationships with his/her offspring in the old ages.

A mole on the left side means this would happen to sons while one on the right means this would happen to daughters.

Left and right dimples — These points are crucial to a person's luck in an agriculture-oriented society. A mole at either spot means animals kept by the person would die and thereby causing financial loss.

In the modern world it means the person's pets would be sick and that is especially likely to happen at age 64 and 65.

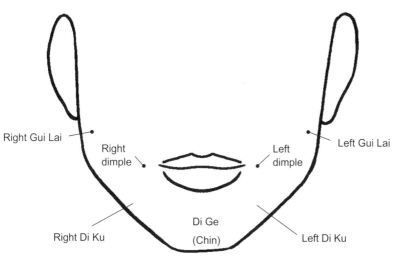

■ *The Cheeks*

The dimples and Fa Ling lines are all on the cheek of the face. As the dimples are covered in the previous section, we will discuss Fa Ling lines in this part.

Fa Ling — Literally, it means law and order in Chinese. A mole on the left Fa ling line means the person's order does not get passed to the subordinate before the age of 30 while one on the right means the same after the age of 30.

Fa Ling lines also refer to the corresponding legs. Therefore a mole on the left Fa Ling means the left leg of the person gets injured easily and one on the right means the same for the right leg. The rest of the cheek does not have any significance to a person's luck. Any mole on the rest of the face can be valued by its aesthetic effects rather than implications on a person's luck.

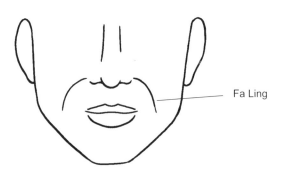

Fa Ling

■ *Mole removal surgery*

Mole is actually a very vague term that could mean flat mole, raised mole, spot, depressed mole, etc. Those light in colour are called spots.

A depressed mole is like a scar with colour. A raised mole could be just concentration of pigments or a large patch with hair. A flat mole could be red or black. A mark is very small and very light in colour. All of these have the same implications from a face-reading point of view. Yet, birthmarks are not significant for a person's luck.

Moles on the face are actually reflecting the internal organs somehow. Thus, surgically removing moles on the face does not truly change a person's luck. Your decision as to whether or not remove your moles should be based on the aesthetic effects only.

32. Features of a sexual pervert

Sexual perverts are cheap men harassing or taking advantages of women willfully or accidentally. More serious cases could turn into indecent assaults or even rapes. One origin of sexual perverts could be that these men have fantasies and intense feelings for women. Yet, they do not dare meet women in socially acceptable ways. They do not dare visit the prostitutes and their desire and sexual energy simply builds up to an unbearable level without any channels to release. When the time and situation allows, they would act out their eccentric fantasies into despicable wrongful behaviour.

From face-reading point of view, we can actually tell if a person has the potential to be a sexual pervert.

1. Thick dense dark eyebrows with "weak" low-spirited eyes — Ancient writings on face-reading mention, "a husband with thick eyebrows growing close to the low-spirited eyes would bring along a whip and kneel in front of his wife." It is because thick dense dark eyebrows mean the person is sexual but cowardly. He is scared of his wife and other women. Moreover, eyes with a "weak" look means he always has sex on his mind and he has mishaps associated with the opposite sex. All these traits account for the person's tendency to act like a pervert — such as peeping at women's private parts, leaning on and sliding his body against women in public transport, or other indecent assaults.

2. Indirect gaze — He never looks straight into people's eyes as he wants to hide his feelings. Even if he likes a woman he does not have to guts to tell her. He cannot get this woman out of his mind and he cannot help but doing something eccentric. He turns into a stalker that follows his subject around and waits for her at her workplace or her home. He always gives others the impression that he is either crazy or a pervert.

3. Small mouth with thick lips — Thick lips mean the person has high sex drive, but small mouth means he is cowardly and does not express himself well. When his sex drive builds up to the intolerable level, he would try to gain sexual pleasure in a perverse way given the time and situation allows. He can never have sexual gratification like others because he is too shy to pursue women and even too cowardly to visit prostitutes.

4. Pale greenish complexion — People with such complexion are imaginative but never put thoughts into action. They are always sneaky and shady. They would even steal women's panties.

5. Wide forehead with pointy chin — This is an inverted triangular face that means too many thoughts without real action. In case such person also has other features implying his sexual nature, he is likely to become an intelligent pervert.

6. Uneasy smile — Obviously thinking about something sexual.

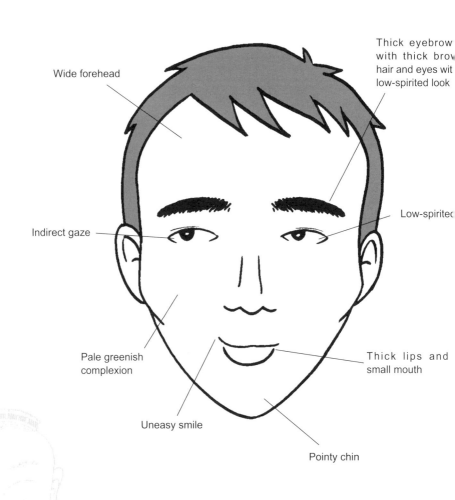

Thick eyebrow with thick brow hair and eyes with low-spirited look

Wide forehead

Low-spirited

Indirect gaze

Pale greenish complexion

Thick lips and small mouth

Uneasy smile

Pointy chin

33. Those who will survive traumatic accidents

There are certain facial features that imply a person can survive serious accidents. Yet, these are not necessary good signs.

Real good signs should mean the person would not even encounter such accidents at all. Therefore, such persons are simply the luckier ones among those with bad luck.

The key reading points for such people are the eyebrows, the eyes, and the presence of auxiliary life line on the palm.

■ *The eyebrows*

1. Dense, thick and dark brow hair — It means the person is likely to have bloodshed incidents.

2. Protruding brow bones with little distance between the eyes and the eyebrows — Protruding brow bones mean the person is short-tempered and impulsive. Little distance between the eyes and the eyebrows means poor interpersonal relationships and frequent arguments, which increases the risk of violent mishaps.

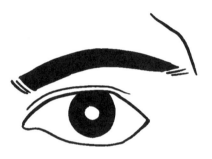

3. Broken eyebrow — It means the person might get injured in the arms or legs due to car accidents.

4. Disorderly and reversely grown brow hair — Messy brow hair implies confused thinking. Reversely grown brow hair means the person does not handle relationships skillfully, including friendship and love relationship. Thus, such person would feel restless and annoyed by relationship matters all the time and they are likely to be involved in gang fights and car crashes.

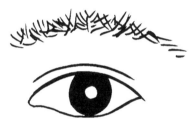

5. Sparsely grown brow hair or no brow hair — Such is a bad sign that the person has court cases and other mishaps all his/her life.

■ *Those who will survive such incidents*

Those having one of the 5 eyebrows just mentioned would encounter bloodshed incidents. Yet, if the person also has high-spirited eyes with clear definition between the eyeballs and the whites, he/she will survive such incidents.

■ *The eyes*

1. **"3-white"** — it means the eyeball is surrounded by the white on 3 sides. It could be the left and right plus white above or below the eyeball. "3-white" implies dangerous incidents and injury. (See Fig 60)

2. **"4-white"** — It means the eyeball is particularly small compared with the whole eye. Big eyeballs mean the person is gentle and virtuous while small eyeballs mean the person is ruthless and cruel. Those with "4-white" are likely to be involved in dangerous incidents and unnatural death. (See Fig 61)

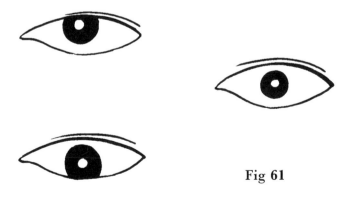

Fig 61

Fig 60

3. Protruding eyes — Protruding eyes on a round face mean the person is talkative and such is not a sign of serious assault. Yet, protruding eyes on a skinny pointy face mean the person is likely to encounter dangerous incidents and injury.

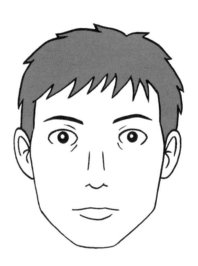

■ *Those who will survive such incidents*

A person with either "3-white", "4-white" eyes, or protruding eyes on a skinny face should engage in charitable activities more often. Charity and other virtuous behaviour help convert and refine the person's temperament. He/she might resolve the predestined danger this way.

The palm

A person with an auxiliary life line running parallel to the line of longevity would encounter life threatening danger. Yet, he/she would survive it.

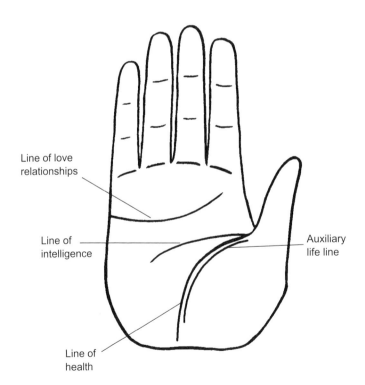

Line of love relationships

Line of intelligence

Auxiliary life line

Line of health

34. Read the voice

The voice of a person has a lot to do with the person's luck. You can judge his/her good luck, bad luck, wealth and poverty from his/her voice.

The voice that originates from the abdominal cavity is of top quality. Such person has high spirit and endless years of luck and fortune. He/she can also resolve problems and become a highly successful wealthy person.

The voice that originates from the thoracic cavity is of mediocre quality. Such person has so-so luck but he/she does not have to worry about food and shelter. He/she is likely to be in the middle class.

The voice that originates from the throat is of low quality. Such person never takes things seriously and he gives up immediately when difficulty arises. He is likely to be broke all his/her life without any major achievement. Yet, a weak voice is actually a good sign for women as it means they can rely on their husbands and let their husbands have say in family matters. The only drawback is that such women might have poor health.

Moreover, from face-reading point of view, a man should sound like a man while a woman should sound like a woman.

A man with a woman's voice means the person is narrow minded and is not suitable for outdoor jobs. He also thinks like woman and he is gentle, thoughtful, has artistic talents and cares about little details. He is likely to worry all the time and as he lacks vital energy ("Qi" in Chinese medical terms) he might live short.

A woman with a man's voice has the bravery and capability of a man. Yet, such woman usually does not have good marriage luck. She might get married three times and still not settling down. The ancient documents say, "why did this woman get married 3 times? She either has fine straight hair hanging down from her hair line, or she has a man's voice."

Loud voice is also a good sign. No matter the person is in the government, agriculture, industry or commerce sector, a loud voice ensures his/her success. It is also a sign of longevity. A senior person with a loud voice must have lots of luck and joy to come. Yet, an old person with a weak voice might have chronic disease or too much to worry about, such as disgraceful sons and daughters or he/she cannot take care of him/herself.

Loud voice should also be clear. A coarse loud voice is not a very good sign as such person is likely to work hard for the money without a break all his/her life (even though he/she would accumulate wealth after all).

A man with a very weak or no voice is the worst sign as he is cowardly and indecisive. He scares too much.

A woman with a sharp squeaky voice is the worst sign as the ancient documents say, "a woman with wide jawbones or a squeaky voice will stay alone in her bedroom." That means the woman is incompatible with her husband in terms of luck and has poor relationship with her husband.

A sharp squeaky voice means she is impatient, miserly and calculating. She does not want to lose or give up anything for her husband. Her attempt to save little always ends up costing her much.

To conclude, a good voice should be loud, clear and sustaining. A bad voice is short, sharp, coarse or no voice at all.

35. Read the walking posture

Besides reading the face and the palm, Chinese face-reading also includes walking, sitting, eating and talking features. An ancient face-reading document says, "Walk like the wind, sit like a bell, stand like a pine tree, eat like a wolf, talk like the thunder: all have their own virtues."

Walking posture is one element of internal reading. It is even more important to a person's luck than the palm and the face. You can tell a person's general luck and luck of wealth by reading his/her walking posture.

■ *Good signs*

Walking like the wind — Such person walks fast with big steps but without waving his/her arms too much. He/she acts fast, is decisive and efficient. He/she must have major achievements.

Walking slowly — This is also a good sign of longevity and luck. Such person walks slowly with small steps. His/her upper torso is still when he/she walks, like a big boulder sliding on the ground. Such person is calm, optimistic and carefree all his/her life. He/she would not panic in front of major frustrations. His/her calmness brings him/her good luck while his/her gentleness brings him/her health and longevity.

Walking not too fast and not too slow — Appropriate

229

speed and sturdy steps in walking means the person has a "middle-of-the-road" kind of luck. He/she has few mishaps and does not have to worry about food and shelter.

■ Bad signs

Snake steps — The person walks like a snake with obviously shaking movements to the left and right. He/she is flamboyant and unserious. Even though he/she can be wealthy, his/her ever-changing thoughts make his/her love life highly unstable. Guys with such walking posture will have poor marriage luck while women with such walking posture might become prostitutes.

Bird steps — The person walks with jumpy little steps like a bird. Kids and the elderly walking like that have good luck as it means the person is full of energy with innocent thinking. Elderly people reverting to childish behaviour are actually considered a good sign in Chinese face reading. Yet, an adult with such walking posture is impractical and unserious. He/she breaks promises, changes his/her mind every minute, and is unlikely to be successful. Even though his/her family might be rich, he/she would dissipate all the wealth pretty soon.

Hanging ankles — A person who walks with his/her ankles not touching the ground aims high but never works from the fundamentals. He/she takes short cuts all the time.

Even though he/she might get rich at a certain point of his/ her life, he/she is likely to lose everything at the end. An ancient document says, "Walking with the ankles not touching the ground, he will lose all the land and has to flee abroad."

Head lowered — A man who walks with his neck bending forward always has worries on his mind. He is pessimistic, self indulged, but cowardly and lack of stamina. He ends up complaining about his talent not being discovered all his life without having any achievement.

Wolf steps — Such person lowers his/her head and turns around frequently when he/she walks. Use care when you meet such person as he/she is incredulous, cunning and paranoid about being harmed because he/she has the intention to harm others.

Head leaning forward — The person walks like he/she is always in a hurry with his/her head leaning ahead of the body. Such person is short tempered and impatient. He/she makes quick but thoughtless decisions. Even though he/she might get rich at one point of his/her life, he/she would end up losing everything. An ancient document says, "Head ahead of the body, the person gets rich but not for long."

Waving arms — A person who walks with big arm waving movements is innocent in thinking, energetic and helpful. Yet, he/she is also insensitive and offends people all the time. That is why he/she would not be successful.

Hands on the back — A person who walks with his/her hands on the back is pessimistic and worrying. Old people who walk with such posture look leisurely but they are actually lonely. Young people with such posture are too careful in handling things, lack of self confidence, and too afraid of failure.

■ *Steps*

Those who walk with the toes pointing straight ahead are normal. They act what they think.

Toes pointing outwards — The person is an extrovert in the heart but without the real capacity to be an extrovert.

Toes pointing inwards — The person is an introvert.

Women walking like a man — No matter they walk naturally like a man or they fake it, such women act fast and impulsively. Yet, it does not necessarily mean they are careless and rude. It could be that they simply do not want to hold on to issues for too long. Read also if such women have a man's face or not. Women who walk like a man without a man's face are just careless and rude. Women who walk like man with a man's face are going to be hugely successful.

Section 4

Resolving Bad Luck

36. Dyeing hair

Hair colour should go well with your birthday to enhance your luck. Dyeing the wrong hair can actually adversely affect your luck. We categorize birthdays to fall into Cold Season, Hot Season and Neutral Season.

Cold Season — Those whose birthdays fall between 8th August and 6th March are said to be Cold Season people with more Yin influence. They should dye their hair yellowish green, green, red, orange or purple to enhance their thoughts and luck.

Hot Season — Those whose birthdays fall between 6th May and 8th August are said to be Hot Season people with more Yang influence. They should dye their hair white, blonde, platinum blonde, black, gray or blue to enhance their thoughts and luck.

Neutral Season — Those whose birthdays fall between 6th March and 6th May are said to be Neutral Season people. As they are born to a mild season, they go well with all 5 elements. Yet, Metal and Water would give them even better luck. They should then dye their hair white, blonde, platinum blonde, black, gray or blue.

Originally, colours do little to a person's luck. However, as the hair covers the top of the skull where a major pressure point Bai Hui is located, the colour of the hair directly affects the energy received through Bai Hui into the brain. Different colours are classified into the 5 elements and dyeing your hair to the colour that complements your predisposition would induce good thinking.

On the other hand, dyeing your hair the wrong colour might hinder your luck. For instance, a Cold Season person dyeing his/her hair in cold toned colours (such as white, blonde, platinum blonde, black, gray or blue) would reinforce the Yin energy he/she was born with. The reinforced Yin energy makes him/her extremely passive in character and that would affects his/her luck. As those Cold Season people were born in autumn or winter seasons when the temperature was low and the Yin energy was strong. They might feel insecure. Adding warm toned colours on hair brings back the balance of Yin and Yang and makes them more active. Using cool toned colours on hair does the opposite.

Similarly, as those Hot Season people have strong Yang energy, using warm toned colours (such as yellowish green, green, red, orange or purple) would make them even more short tempered, impatient and lack of stamina. Using cool toned colours can balance out the Yang energy they were born with. Neutral Season people were born to a mild weather and they usually have balanced Yin and Yang energy, or slightly on the Yang side. Even though they would have the best luck if they dye their hair with cool toned colours, dyeing the wrong colours is not going to affect their luck too much.

■ *The colours of 5 elements*

Wood — yellowish green, green

Fire — red, orange, purple

Earth — earthy tones like beige, yellow and brown

Metal — white, gold, silver

Water — black, gray, blue

■ *Premature gray hair*

Gray hair all over at an early age usually means remote relationship with the father, or that the father is unable to help the person.

By "remote relationship" I mean the person has to live away from his/her father since an early age, either because of geographical separation or his/her father dies early. The father might also be too weak and vain to have enough success to pass on to the sons and daughters.

In case you already have gray head all over, you can dye it a colour that complements your birthday just like what I said earlier. If you strong resist to the idea of dyeing your hair, you can also put on caps or hats of the right colour for similar effects.

37. The risk of accidents associated with water

Some people are especially prone to accidents associated with water. Before you jump into the sea make sure you know if you are one of them.

■ Water disaster index

1. Particularly thick eyebrows (the person has accidents and mishaps all his/her life) ─ 4 points

2. Thick and tough hair ─ 3 points

3. Thick and dense facial hair ─ 3 points

4. Dense brow hair covering a mole (the person has mishaps associated with water all his/her life) ─ 5 points

5. Eyes with low-spirited look ─ 3 points

6. The line of longevity is broken or there is a cross pattern right on the line (a life threatening incident would occur to the person before the age of 30 if it happens to the left hand. The same incident would occur after the age of 30 if the broken line or cross pattern happens to the right hand.) (See Fig 62, 63) — 5 points

7. A short line running parallel to the line of longevity. (See Fig 64). It means person encounters life threatening events. — 5 points

8. Born in winter (born with much Water energy, should avoid water) — 2 points

9. zodiac in conflicts with the star god presiding over that year (i.e. the years of your zodiac or the years conflicting your zodiac) — 3 points

10. Born in the year of Pig, Rat or Ox (with much Water energy) — 2 points

11. A green, dark or black patch in the chin (i.e. a mishap will happen soon) — 7 points

12. The lips are green or dark in colour (i.e. a mishap will happen soon) — 7 points

13. Gray complexion on the face (i.e. a mishap will happen soon) — 7 points

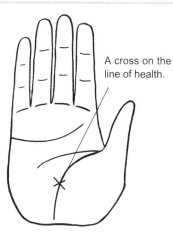

A cross on the line of health.

Fig 62

A broken line of health

Fig 63

A short line is parallel of the line of health

Fig 64

If you score more than 12 points, you should refrain from swimming or use extra care when you are in water. Risky water sports like diving and water skiing should be avoided altogether.

Even if you don't score any point, you should still be careful and be prepared before you do any exercise.

■ Resolving the risks

If you score more than 12 points but you really want to swim, you can resolve the risks by using Feng Shui.

A proverb says, "first destiny, second luck and third Feng Shui." Put a rock, a ceramic item or a piece of jade (or other items made of natural stones or gems) in the northern most point of your house to suppress the Water from the north. Then put something red in colour in the southern most point to enhance Fire to counteract the Water. You can take half of the scores away if you do this.

38. Body piercing

Many people ask me if ear or brow piecing affects a person's luck. Actually all scars left on the body would affect luck somehow. Yet, some areas are more crucial to luck than others.

The ears — They govern luck from age 0 to 14. Ear piercing will not affect a person's luck after the age of 14.

The eyebrows — Piercing on the eyebrows are more influential as they are the areas of friendship and sibling relationship. They also govern luck from age 31 to 34. Thus, having the eyebrows pierced before age 31 would affect the luck in those years. The eyebrows also refer to the arms. Such piercing would mean higher possibility of getting injured in the arms.

The nose — It is the location of luck of wealth — nose tip refer to stable income while the nose wings refer to unstable wealth. Piercing on the nose would affect a person's luck of wealth. Besides directly affecting the luck from age 48 to 50, such piercing also affects the luck at age 20, 29, 38 and 47.

The lips — The upper lip governs love while the lower lip governs sex. Therefore piercing on the upper lip hinders the development of love while one on the lower lip hinders the enjoyment of sex.

The tongue — It means language and piercing on the tongue means problems in expressing him/herself clearly and poor credibility.

The nipples ─ The breast is for feeding infants. In the ancient world, people read a woman's breast to see if she is promiscuous, fertile or noble. As breast feeding is less common nowadays due to the popularity of instant milk powder, the primary function of the breast fades out. It is now commonly viewed as an erogenous zone.

People have their nipples pierced to draw attention and to highlight their sexiness. Thus, you can imply they must be passionate, sexy and sentimental.

There is actually no relevance on men having their nipples pierced from face-reading point of view.

The naval ─ It is the area of offspring and piercing in the naval could affect fertility and relationship with children. Yet, as most naval rings are pierced onto the skin around the naval but not in the naval, the effect would not be that serious.

39. Counteracting against bad facial features

Some people were born with bad luck with intrinsic shortcomings in personality.

It is extremely difficult for them to change as firstly, sometimes they don't think they have a problem; secondly, they don't want to change even if they admit they have a problem; finally, they don't know what they can do.

Let me tell you what you can do in this article.

■ *Pointy skull with narrow forehead; not noble material*

A pointy protrusion at the Bai Hui pressure point on top of the skull means the person has strong self esteem and does not admit his failure. A narrow forehead means the person is not intelligent and is poor in analysis.

Such person values him/herself too much without admitting he/she is not a bright smart person. He/she is deemed to fail on big projects and doesn't even care to lay his/her hands on small or less important projects. He/she is likely to be broke all his/her life and end up without a proper shelter and dying of hunger.

Resolving the bad luck:

If you have such skull and forehead, you should start acting practically and work from the lowest position to compensate your lack of intelligence with diligence.

You should also focus in only one specific area so that even though you might not be rich, you can still make enough money for food and shelter without any problem.

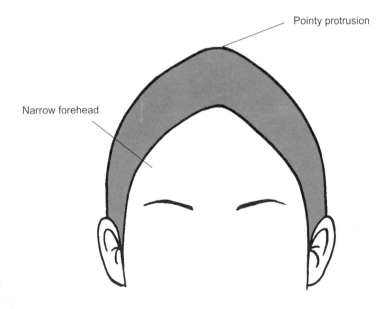

Pointy protrusion

Narrow forehead

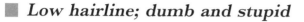

■ *Low hairline; dumb and stupid*

Low hairline means a short forehead which implies the person does not think very swiftly. He/she is also stubborn and insistent without taking any advice. Therefore, he/she has poor interpersonal relationship and is hard to get along with.

Resolving the bad luck:

Shave the hair along the hairline to raise the hairline. Meanwhile, remind yourself why you are doing this. After you do this repeatedly, the shaved hair might stop growing and you can rectify your shortcomings.

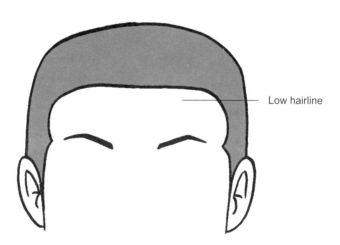

Low hairline

Thick dense eyebrows growing too close to the eyes

Such person usually has eyes with a low spirited look. He/she is cowardly, miserly and calculating. He/she is scared of doing anything more than he/she is paid to. He/she never wants to give but always wants to take. How can such person be successful?

Resolving the bad luck:

Pluck the brow hair growing close to the eyes and at the same time, remind yourself why you are doing this. Tell yourself to let go, take it easy, be more generous. Then start training your eyes to have more spirit. After a long time, your character and your appearance would change. That's what meant by "the face originates from the heart."

■ *Low nose bridge*

It means lack of self confidence. No matter how hard he/she works, he/she becomes indecisive and hesitant when it comes to crucial issues. That could miss all the opportunities.

Resolving the bad luck:

Most people with low nose bridge have fleshy cheekbones. Such cheekbones imply help from others. Therefore, such people should cooperate with someone powerful and wealthy to develop business, or follow someone else's decisions to improve their own luck.

■ *Connected eyebrows; too insistent*

People think those with their two eyebrows connected are narrow minded. That is not true.

Actually, they are simply too insistent and cannot let go. Any minor little discontent, unhappiness or frustration will stay on their mind forever. They are likely to bring home those unhappy issues and therefore give others a narrow minded impression.

Resolving the bad luck:

Pluck the brow hair at the centre to separate the two eyebrows. Meanwhile, remind yourself why you are doing it. Tell yourself to let go, and not to insist too much. Do it repeatedly to change your pessimistic attitude.

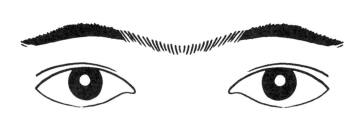

■ *Messy brow hair and fluffy outer brow end*

Fluffy outer brow end means the person cannot accumulate wealth and he/she loves to gamble. Messy brow hair means the person is confused at heart and is not very intelligent. Such gambler without the brain is going to lose whenever he/she gambles. Besides gambling, the person takes the same approach in business and always wants to use smallest investment to make major profit. He/she aims high without the capacity and he/she never starts from the fundamentals. Therefore, such person is unlikely to have any achievement.

Resolving the bad luck:

Trim the brow hair. At the same time remind yourself to be practical and start from the fundamentals.

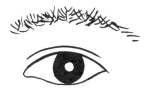

■ Eyes with "weak" look

Such people look like they are asleep or drunk when they are not. They always look fatigue and low spirited. They start something without finishing it. Their lack of stamina and patience makes them unable to encounter any problem. They are unlikely to have achievement because they are hesitant and indecisive. Sexual scandals, triangular love relationships and other improper love affairs would happen to them always.

Resolving the bad luck:

Do Qi Gong with motions such as Tai Chi or Liu Tong Quan to strengthen the Qi and clear the internal organs.

When your mind is clearer, you would have a stronger look to the eyes. When you have stronger look, you will have better analytical power and will be more likely to succeed.

■ *Pointy chin*

It means poor luck in the final years and remote spousal relationship. The person does not take care of the family and kids and does not want to stay at home. He/she is unlikely to settle down.

Resolving the bad luck:

Get married to a partner with the same pointy chin. As the two of you have the same personality, you can travel around the world without settling down.

You should save money for the old ages as such chin means bad luck after the age of 60. Having some money would save you from being lonely and broke in the final years.

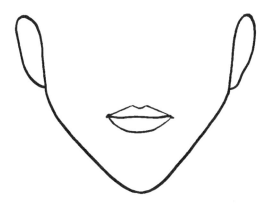

40. Length of the hair

You can actually enhance your interpersonal skills and love luck by keeping the right hairstyle to complement your face.

■ *Long hair*

It is good for those with square face and protruding jawbones. As such woman is stubborn and strong in character, she might not be able to enjoy the success of her husband. Growing long hair adds more gentleness to the image, which can enhance her interpersonal relationship and love luck.

Long hair also goes well with round face.

Round face belongs to the category of Water in the 5 elements. Hair belongs to the category of Wood and it can balance out the Water energy that is too strong in a round face. It would improve her thinking. Thus, long hair would surely benefit those in the show business or art scene with a round face. Those are not in such businesses are not affected by long hair.

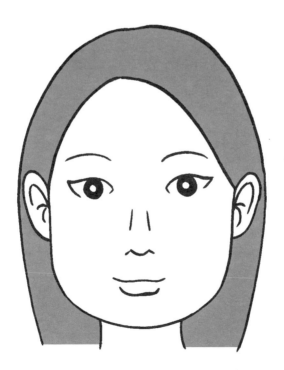

■ *Short hair*

Those with an oval face should grow short hair as such hair highlights the beautiful shape of the face and enhances their attractiveness.

This is especially true for those in the show business, or those engaged in occupations that involve frequent meetings with strangers.

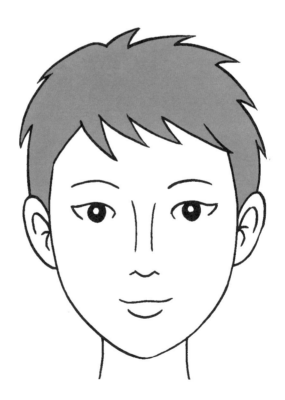

Short hair goes well with a short face. As long hair will accentuate the shortness of the face, growing short hair is the only option.

Short hair also brings out the facial features and improves the appearance. Both interpersonal relationship and love luck would be enhanced afterwards.

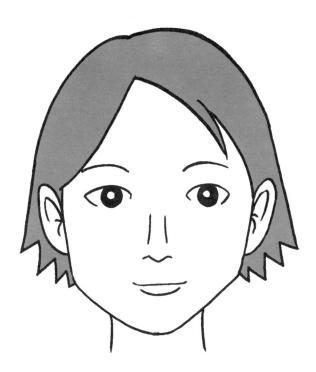

41. Wearing spectacles for luck

Many fortune tellers ask people to wear glasses to block out unwanted love affairs, mishaps and unnecessary injury. In truth, simply wearing a pair of glasses could barely help improve your luck. You need to know why you wear glasses, what mishaps and what kind of bad luck you are trying to block out. Then you need to use care to avoid such from happening.

Basically, spectacles can be used for blocking out four types of bad luck:

■ *Unwanted love affairs*

Big eyes with big eyeballs — Women with such eyes attract unwanted pursuits all their lives. Big eyeballs mean she is kind, gentle and sympathetic towards others. Big eyes mean she is innocent, gullible and loves asking questions. She is likely to be cheated by liars. Such woman should wear glasses in those years governed by the eyes (i.e. age 35 to 40).

Small tearful eyes — Most people with such eyes are women. Such women are likely to be involved in love triangle and have to overcome many frustrations in relationships. They usually suffer from break-ups or divorce if they get married before the age of 35. Their marriage luck would be better if they get married from age 35 to 40. Thus, those with such eyes and have married before the age of 35 should

wear glasses in hope of reversing the bad luck.

Sagging eyelids ⸺ Such eyes look sleepy all the time as the upper eyelids cover the top half of the eyes. (See Fig 217) Again, such eyes are more commonly seen on women. Such women are usually confused in love relationship and their rational mind cannot control their sexual desire. They would willfully fall in love with someone regardless of his marital status. Women with such eyes are likely to become prostitutes while men with such eyes are highly sexual. They should wear glasses to block out unwanted sexual encounters.

Eye white with pinkish tint ⸺ Such trait is originally solely seen in men, but I came across some women having such eyes in recent years. Such people would have an exceptionally high chance of falling in love with the opposite sex from age 35 to 40. If they are still single at the time, things would be okay. Yet, if they are married, such affair would lead to divorce, multiple relationships, and associated financial loss. Thus, such people should wear glasses in those years to block out possible affairs.

Fig 217

Bloodshed incidents

People with protruding eyes and a skinny build are likely to have bloodshed incidents. They should wear glasses in those years governed by the eyes to block out possible mishaps. This also applies to "3-white" and "4-white" eyes.

Court cases

Ferocious eyes — You can literally feel the ferocity of a person from such eyes. He/she is extremely impulsive and short tempered. Even though he/she might be well educated and has excellent tolerance, he/she would lose all his/her patience in those years governed by the eyes (i.e. age 35 to 40). The person is likely to get involved in gang fights or associated court cases. He/she should wear glasses in those years.

Glossy eyes — An ancient face-reading document says, "a person with glossy eyes must either be a burglar or a cunning person."

Glossy eyes are filled with tears suddenly and can be read in two ways. The person with glossy eyes and a smiling face might just start dating someone he/she loves and the relationship is going fine. Of course, he/she does not have to wear glasses in such case.

On the other hand, the person with such eyes without a

smile should beware of any court cases or injury. He/she should wear glasses. If the person has glossy eyes and a sad face, he/she must have already got involved in the court case and waiting for the trial. Wearing glasses does not help much at this point.

Fraud

Eyes with a low-spirited look mean the person is slow in thinking and not intelligent. He/she is gullible and is especially likely to be a fraud victim in those years governed by the eyes. He/she should wear glasses in those years.

Colours of the frames

Cold Season people — Those born between 8th August and 6th March should wear plastic frames in yellowish green, green, red, orange or purple.

Hot Season people — Those born between 6th May and 8th August.

Neutral Season people — Those born between 6th March and 6th May.

Both Hot and Neutral Season people should wear metallic frame in white, gold, silver, black, gray or blue.

42. The likelihood of being haunted

Most people don't want to see things that they are not supposed to see. Actually the likelihood of person seeing spiritual beings or related phenomenon can be calculated according to the person's facial features, birthday and the Feng Shui of his/her home. For the sake of easy calculation, now I put down such factors into a scoring system. Higher scores mean you have more chance of seeing the supernatural beings.

▪ Scoring system

1. Imbalanced eyeballs (3 points) — When you look straight ahead, if one of your eyes is slightly skewed to the left or right and not right at the centre of the eye, you have imbalanced eyeballs. As the gaze is not focused in such case, you might meet spiritual beings.

2. Eyes with low-spirit look (3 points) — Such person looks like he/she is sleepy or drunk even when he/she is not. His/her lack of vital energy (Qi) means he/she has more chance to see ghosts.

3. Thick eyebrows with thick brow hair growing close to the eyes (3 points) — This also means a lack of vital energy. The case is even worse if the person also has weak gentle gaze. He/she is cowardly and he/she would create a ghost in his/her mind when there isn't one.

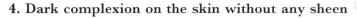

4. Dark complexion on the skin without any sheen — (**2 points**) The person is having a low in terms of luck.

5. Dark patch at Xin Tang (2 points) — It means he/she has bad luck at that moment. Xin Tang is also a location of vital energy accumulation. A dark patch there means the person would bump into bad events all the time.

6. Small mouth (1 point) — The person is cowardly and would get nervous with the slightest irrelevant clues. His/her fright suppresses his/her Yang energy.

7. Particularly long middle finger (1 point) — A person with long middle finger tends to enjoy retreating alone into some quiet places.

8. Zodiac of the Earth element (1 point) — Earth means mystery in life. Those born with much Earth energy are more likely to meet supernatural beings. Such zodiacs include Goat, Dog, Ox and Dragon.

9. Born in the months of the Earth element (1 point) — Those born in the 3rd, 6th, 9th and 12th month of the lunar calendar have more Earth energy.

10. Born in the hours of the Earth element (1 point) — Those born between 7 — 9 am, 7 — 9 pm, 1 — 3 am have more Earth energy.

11. The door of your house faces either of the 4 borders of Yin and Yang (2 points) — The directions Southeast, Northwest, Southwest and Northeast are the intrinsic and extrinsic borders between the real world and the spiritual world. If the entrance door of your house faces directly to either direction, you have more chance to see the ghost.

12. Living in a low-lying area (1 point) — Houses on the mountain are said to be Yang in nature while houses in a low-lying area are said to be Yin in nature as low-lying land absorbs the Yin energy. For your information, ghosts are considered to be Yin in nature while humans are considered to be Yang in nature.

13. Living next to the cemetery plus incompatible land luck (1 point) — Living near a cemetery, by itself, is not a sign of bad luck. Yet, you have to pay attention to the land luck of your geographical location. Those lots with luck "7" having a cemetery in the East; lots with luck "8" having a cemetery in the Southwest; and lots with luck "9" having a cemetery in the North are all considered bad in terms of Feng Shui.

14. Cold Season person wearing black (1 point) — Such person is born between 8th August and 6th March of the following year. Those born between 7th November and 4th February have especially strong Yin energy. Black is the colour of strongest Yin nature. A person with much Yin energy wearing the colour of strongest Yin nature means overwhelming Yin energy.

15. Cold Season person driving a black car (1 point) — The same rhetoric as paragraph 14.

16. Going to places of Yin nature at Yu Lan Festival (1 point) — Yu Lan Festival is the festival of spirits when the gate between the real and supernatural world open. Going to places like low-lying land, basement, wild mountains, sea coast and walking underneath a balcony that day is more likely to see ghosts.

17. Being female (1 point) — As male is considered Yang and female is considered Yin in Chinese belief, females meet supernatural beings more easily. Don't you see it's the female washroom getting haunted, and not the male washroom, in most of the cases?

Now you can sum up your total score. The higher the score, the more likely you would see ghosts.

0-3 points: You can relax as you don't have much karma with ghost.

3-5 points: You are not very likely to see ghosts, unless you are with someone scoring higher than you.

6-8 points: You have a predestined relationship with the spirits and quite a big chance of seeing one.

9 or above: you have even more chance of meeting supernatural beings all the time.

■ *What should I do when I see a ghost?*

To avoid seeing a ghost, it is important to bring along something you can lay your mind on to. For instance, many Chinese wear a jade accessory while Caucasians wear a cross. Buddhists might say a Buddhist prayer while Christians might recite a paragraph from the Bible. All these actions can focus your mind, reinforce the Yang energy in your body and calm your nerves. Of course, you should avoid getting drunk.

■ *Reading the complexion of those being haunted*

You can tell a person is seeing ghosts by reading the colour on the face. There are 3 levels of being haunted:

Level 1 — Dark green colour on the cheeks means the person met the spirits without noticing.

Level 2 — Dark green colour around the mouth means the person met the spirits and he/she knew it.

Level 3 — Dark green colour around the mouth, eyes

with a low-spirited look and a lack of focus. The person seems not registering what he/she sees.

Please note level 3 is actually very similar to a person just survived a major break-up with his/her lover. So do not diagnose him/her as haunted simply by his/her face. A person at level 3 is already in the stage of being seized by spirits and should seek help from professional exorcists immediately. (Please don't call me as I am not such expert.)

N.B. The third month of the lunar calendar roughly spans from 5th April to 6th May. The sixth month of the lunar calendar roughly spans from 8th July to 8th August. The ninth month of the lunar calendar is from 8th October to 7th November while the twelfth month is from 5th January to 4th February.

43. Growing facial hair for luck

It looks like a section solely devoted to male readers. Yet, you, as his other half, should also know if he should be growing his facial hair.

Those men with dry yellow facial hair grown messily should not grow any. Similarly, those with beard that splits into the two sides like a pair of scissors should not grow any either.

Beard should be soft, shiny and widely grown. In case your facial is hard and thick, it's better that it is also curly.

Growing facial for luck is because the person has shortcomings on his face from face-reading point of view.

Growing facial hair can cover up or rectify the shortcomings and thereby enhancing his luck.

If you do not have any shortcomings on your face, you should simply consider growing facial hair from a purely aesthetic point of view.

Facial hair to tackle different short-comings

Exposed nostrils — The nose is the location of the luck of wealth. Nostrils slightly exposed mean the person has luck of unstable income. Yet, nostrils totally facing the front mean the person has major financial losses all the time and is unable to accumulate wealth before the age of 50.

Growing moustache helps cover up the nostrils and thereby minimizing financial losses.

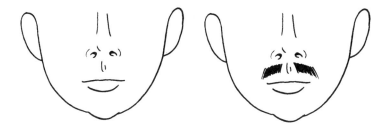

Unobvious philtrum — Philtrum is the vertical groove between the nose and the upper lip.

A good philtrum should be deep, wide and long.

A shallow unobvious philtrum means the person has poor relationship with sons and daughters.

Growing moustache but shaving the philtrum makes it look like a deep wide philtrum and that would change the luck.

Unobvious Fa Ling — Fa Ling lines are the laugh lines connecting the nose wings to the area next to the mouth corners. Fa Ling literally means law and order in Chinese.

Unobvious Fa Ling lines mean the person's order does not reach his/her subordinate and he/she cannot be a good leader.

Such person would have no problem if his/her job does not require management of staff. Yet, a man in the managerial level with unobvious Fa Ling lines may try growing moustache so that the Fa Ling lines look more obvious.

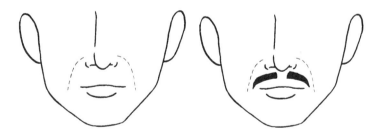

Flat Fu Er — It means the person's jawbones are not obvious.

Unobvious jawbones not only mean bad luck in the late years but also imply the person has no stamina to face difficulties and lacks strong will to survive in the hard times.

Growing sideburns on the jaws helps define the jaws better and improve the luck.

Sharp pointy chin — It means bad relationship in the family and poor luck in the old ages.

Growing sideburns and beard makes the chin look wider and helps improve luck in a long run.

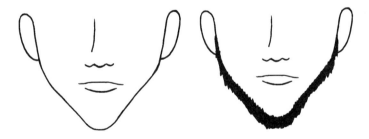

Receding chin — It means the person is impulsive and short tempered. He/she acts fast but without stamina to sustain the energy. He/she is ready to give up when problems arise. Such person also makes thoughtless decisions without knowing the consequences and is unlikely to success.

Growing beard helps change the luck and in a long run, he might be able to change his impulsive personality.

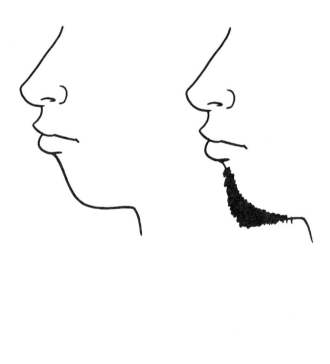